Jerome Bruner has been involved for many years in studying the development of human capacities – social, intellectual, emotional, linguistic. His work has taken him into nurseries, schools, playgroups, villages in Africa, hospitals, and highly technical laboratories. Born in New York in 1915, he was educated at Duke and Harvard Universities, and was later Guggenheim Fellow at St John's College, Cambridge. His career has combined research, practice, and policy. He has been Professor of Psychology at Harvard, later Watts Professor of Psychology at Oxford, and is presently Sloan Foundation Fellow at Harvard. In both Britain and America he has served on various public commissions concerned with the problems of human development, the most recent of which was the Oxford Preschool Research Group on whose work this book is based.

Oxford Preschool Research Project

1 *Under Five in Britain* Jerome Bruner
2 *Childwatching at Playgroup and Nursery School* Kathy Sylva, Carolyn Roy and Marjorie Painter
3 *Children and Minders* Bridget Bryant, Miriam Harris and Dee Newton
4 *Children and Day Nurseries* Caroline Garland and Stephanie White
5 *Working with Under Fives* David Wood, Linnet McMahon and Yvonne Cranstoun
6 *Parents' Preschool Involvement* Teresa Smith

Under Five in Britain

Jerome Bruner

First published in 1980 by
Grant McIntyre Ltd
39 Great Russell Street
London WC1B 3PH

Hardback: ISBN 0 86216 000 6
Paperback: ISBN 0 86216 001 4

Bruner, Jerome Seymour
    Under five in Britain. – (Oxford Preschool
    Research Project; 1)
    1. Day care centers – England – Oxfordshire
    2. Day care centers – Great Britain – Case
    studies
    I. Title   II. Series
    362.7′1   HV861.G620/

    ISBN 0-86216-000-6
    ISBN 0-86216-001-4 Pbk

Text set in 10/12 pt VIP Times,
printed and bound in Great Britain at The Pitman Press, Bath

Contents

In memory of Jack Tizard
and in appreciation of
Barbara Tizard

Foreword by Jack Wrigley

In 1971, when a massive expansion of nursery education in Britain was proposed, there was relatively little easily available evidence to suggest how best this should be done. Consequently the Department of Education and Science and the Scottish Education Department initiated a programme of research on nursery education to answer practical questions about provision and to study the effects of expansion. The Educational Research Board of the Social Science Research Council saw the need for a complementary research programme concerned as well with some more fundamental issues which covered the whole range of preschool education.

The work was coordinated in the Department of Education and Science by a management committee on which the Schools Council and SSRC were represented. The original idea, that SSRC should concentrate on fundamental research while DES funded more policy oriented and practical work, proved too simple. What quickly emerged was a view that much of the fundamental work on preschool children had already been carried out. What was lacking was the dissemination of that knowledge and its implementation in the field. Within SSRC a preschool working group was given the task of commissioning projects, and the work of the Oxford Preschool Research Group, under Professor Bruner, reported in this series of publications, was the main element in the first phase of the SSRC programme.

Professor Bruner had already accomplished distinguished fundamental work in this field and was therefore well placed to make the point of the need for dissemination and implementation. Despite the many changes in the economic and political scene in the 1970s the original gap in knowledge remains important and the results of the SSRC research programme will do much to fill the gap. In particular, Professor Bruner's work in Oxfordshire has great value for the rest of the country. The publications of the Oxford Preschool Research Group, together with the results from other participants in the programme, will help give a firmer base on which to build for the future.

Jack Wrigley
Chairman
SSRC Educational Research
Board Panel on
Accountability in
Education

London, 1979

Acknowledgements

There are many people to whom I am greatly indebted for help in the work that has led to this book. Chief among them are the members of the Oxford Preschool Research Group, which I directed from 1975 to 1979. They included Dr Harry Judge, as Associate Director, and Miriam Harris, in her role as Project Administrator. The following were involved in planning and conducting the research: Dr Kathy Sylva, Carolyn Roy, Majorie Painter, Bridget Bryant, Miriam Harris, Dee Newton, Caroline Garland, Stephanie White, Dr David Wood, Dr Linnet McMahon, Yvonne Cranstoun, Teresa Smith, Dr Judy Bradley, Terry End, Avril Holmes, Martha Kempton, Virginia Makins, Philippa Maxwell, Sue North and Kirsteen Tate.

I am most grateful for secretarial help to Joanna Boyce, Jan Macnish and Sasha Metaxas.

The following busy people kindly gave their time to serve as members of our management committee: Geoffrey Caston, John Garne, John Llewellyn, Professor Jack Wrigley, and Dr Harry Judge as Chairman. A planning seminar during the early development of the project was particularly valuable. It included Geoffrey Caston, Dr Judy Dunn, Professor A. H. Halsey, Miriam Harris, Dr Harry Judge, Dr Kathy Sylva, George Smith, Teresa Smith, Gail Taylor, Dr Barbara Tizard and Dr David Wood.

Liaison with the Social Science Research Council was greatly helped by Arabella Pope and Glyn Davies.

Many people in Oxfordshire were very kind in aiding our research and in giving us counsel. Among them Dr John Coe, David Hawley, John Garne (the Chief Education Officer), John Llewellyn (the Director of Social Services), Lady Phelps–Brown and Joan Lawrence were particularly helpful. I wish especially to thank a group of tutors from the Oxfordshire Pre-school Playgroups Association, Sanchia Austin, Avril Holmes, Ann Thompson and Chris Wells, for their cooperation in a seminar early in the life of the project. Kirsteen Tate undertook a study of BBC policy related to child care and nursery education: she greatly improved our understanding of the problems of dissemination.

My colleagues in the Oxford Preschool Research Group have been particularly helpful during the writing of this book, and I am most grateful for their comments and criticisms, large and small. I owe a special debt to several friends who read and criticized various drafts of the manuscript in preparation. Among them are Tessa Blackstone, Barbara Tizard, Helen Fraser, Grant McIntyre and Burton Rosner. Many others have provided me with useful ideas and equally useful corrections of my interpretations of the British scene, and I acknowledge these with gratitude.

Finally, this book is dedicated to two scholar-activists who have made an enormous contribution to our understanding of the care of children, Jack and Barbara Tizard. Professor Jack Tizard died in August 1979; Dr Barbara Tizard carries on. I am indebted to them both, both intellectually and personally. We mourn the death of a man whose gifts and passions are so needed while the care of children is in jeopardy in a beleaguered Britain.

Preface and prologue

This volume is about the care of children under five in Britain, particularly outside the home – and with ways and means of improving that care in the years ahead. It is based on a three-year inquiry into the provision of such care, carried out from 1975 to 1978. Our inquiry concentrated principally upon the major community institutions that care for the young – nursery schools, playgroups, day-care centres, and childminders. But we were inevitably brought to consider as well matters of family and personal values that lie beyond the usual scope of the social sciences. What is good care? Social scientists are not the judges of how children should be brought up. Nor should they be. Yet it does not take deep probing to recognize that the modern family is beset by difficulties in finding the care outside the home that many parents feel they need. The difficulties often arise not within the family but in the broader community – and they reverberate back into the family in a highly personal way. While the issues are economic, social, and political, their impact on family life and the life of children is personal, value-laden, and highly controversial. So while our task during the three years of the Project was focused on the care of young children away from home in Britain – particularly its pitfalls and opportunities – we have been forced to raise questions about fundamental values for which we have no answers. Our belief is that the questions will themselves be of value.

The work of the project – it became known as the Oxford Preschool Research Group – was financed by the Educational Research Board of the Social Science Research Council. It was commissioned during the buoyant period in 1975 when it was thought that at last Britain was about to launch on a major expansion of preschool care. Mrs Thatcher, then Secretary of State for Education and Science, had just issued a White Paper, *Education: a Framework for Expansion* (1972) which proposed an increase in State-financed care for the under-fives in general and for those socially 'at risk' in particular. SSRC was asked to stimulate research that would ensure a sensible pattern of expansion and earmarked special funds so that it could get on with the task. But, as I shall relate in a bit more detail later, it was not at all clear how to provoke research that could in fact guide expansion. A working weekend in the country was arranged at Ware to which the 'leading figures' in child research were invited, these previously having been winnowed out in a survey of research conducted for the Council by Barbara Tizard. The objective of the meeting was to choose a focus for research in support of the soon to be expanded system of nursery care.

There were several presuppositions that were prevalent but implicit at the working weekend in Ware. The first was that *research was needed* either on what put children at risk or what helped them to develop more robustly. The second presupposition was that a decision about *what* research was needed was to come from researchers and research administrators in consultation with those responsible at the highest level for the conduct of preschool education and care. In consequence, the meeting was attended not only by the leaders of the research community and members of the SSRC Educational Research Board, but also by representatives of Her Majesty's Inspectorate and the Department of Education and Science. There were no representatives of the community or of the various voluntary organizations operating in the field – though an educational journalist was in attendance, not so much as a substitute for grass-roots 'community activists' as an assurance that the proceedings would not be behind closed doors. There were no nursery teachers and no playgroup leaders. These two implicit presuppositions were destined to be deeply questioned before ever the Project came into being.

The Council eventually invited me to submit a research

proposal on factors affecting the care of the under-fives away from home. The letter of invitation said:

> One of the Working Group's first decisions was to endorse the recommendation made by the seminar participants, namely that the major part of the available funds should be concentrated on one research team. In considering which centre would be appropriate for the development of the kind of research programme envisaged, the Working Group were very much attracted to Oxford, where there is already a considerable body of research expertise, and where moves are afoot to establish an administrative framework to draw together individuals from a variety of disciplines who have a common interest in educational research.
>
> The kinds of research areas into which the Working Group would like the programmes to fall are as follows:
>
> (i) studies in monitored intervention [i.e., nursery programmes accompanied by studies of their effects];
> (ii) studies of skills, and their development through curricula;
> (iii) multi-disciplinary studies of the structure of curricula and invisible pedagogies in the peer-group, home, and school.
> (iv) studies (socio-political in style) of the community, its organization and 'empowerment' in relation to pre-school provision.
>
> Of course, these areas overlap to a considerable extent and are certainly not intended to be exclusive categories or strict alternatives. The final shape of the programme would depend very much on the particular aspects which you would prefer to concentrate on.

It was a direct expression of the two presuppositions at Ware: that research was needed and that its nature could be decided from above.

Here I must say a word about myself in order to make

clear why my first response to the invitation was to decline it. That may seem a strange thing to do for a Professor of Psychology who had spent the preceding twenty years not only studying the growth of children but also working for better schools and better facilities for the care of the young before they enter school. I am an American who came to Britain in 1972 to occupy a chair in psychology at Oxford. I had been closely associated in America with the founding of Head Start and had been on various White House advisory committees concerned with stimulating and giving shape to research in support of early care. What I had learned was that even when there was ample research available on factors that put young children at risk or that helped them to cope better, it rarely found its way into practice. Was there not already enough research locked up in the learned journals that had *not* been used? Was more of the same needed? Why was dissemination so baffling? Why did all of this compiled knowledge have so little effect on child care practice and policy? That was the question that gave me pause.

It was not that the findings of research were so radical as to require extreme reform policies concerning the redistribution of wealth or a basic redefinition of the family and its responsibilities. There seemed to be extraordinary difficulty in getting accumulated research knowledge about child development into practice even when it seemed *not* to require upheaval in the social or economic order, even when not much change in expenditure was required. Indeed, I had been stunned in the United States at the speed with which resistance had grown up among Head Start teachers to further research on children in their care. I still recall being told by a Head Start supervisor: 'We don't need to be told by research how to bring up our children.'

The proposals of the SSRC were perfectly reasonable. My initial reluctance about getting involved in another research project was the worry that once again the results would travel little beyond the closed circle of the research community. When asked what I would like to do instead, I proposed that we not only *do* research but also explore how research findings get from the research community into the community of practitioners.

Now, several years later, the research is completed. Obviously, one of the main roads into the broader community is to write a book about the findings of the work that will be of interest and help to people involved in caring for the young. That, of course, was planned from the start. But we wanted as well to gear the research itself, while in progress, to the needs of practitioners not only that we might in the end have more apposite things to say, but also that we might better discern how research gets into practice and how it can be helped to get there. There is something very final about a book *after* the project is done! Could we get hold of the dissemination problem a little in advance of the 'final report', so to speak? Not only would we do research on the conduct of childminding, of nursery schools and playgroups, and of all-day nurseries, we would also explore ways of working jointly with them to see how research could be tailored to their needs. That turned out to be an informative if at times an abrasive enterprise. We also convinced Virginia Makins, a wise and experienced educational journalist, to help us think more practically about matters of dissemination while the work was in progress. The usual way researchers go about their business tends to be asymmetrical. The research is formulated (as at Ware) by experts, by 'us', to be applied by 'them', the practitioners. We ask them to turn *our* knowledge into *their* habits. But I am running too far ahead.

One of our earliest decisions (in keeping with our collaborative aim) was to convene a group of experienced researchers and an equally lively group of child care practitioners in Oxfordshire to help us formulate a research strategy. The fortnightly seminars lasted over several months and yielded many rich ideas (how could it have been otherwise with a membership including Barbara Tizard, Judy Dunn, David Wood, Harry Judge, Geoffrey Caston, Kathy Sylva, Marjorie Painter, A. H. Halsey, and others of especially broad experience?) For one thing, we soon learned that little was known about what in fact constituted ordinary preschool care away from home. The literature on preschool care was heavy in presupposition and light in description – at least description of everyday practice. And this led to our first modest but important decision – to have a close look at what in fact goes on in nursery schools and classes, in playgroups, in day nurseries and at the childminders'.

Indeed, the technical literature on early human development in general has surprisingly little to say about the effects of different kinds of preschool experiences on the normal course of growth. In so far as the general literature was relevant, it concerned trouble-factors that interfered with healthy development. There was little to guide the formulation of good practice. The seminar decided, and this was its second basic decision, that our research should place principal emphasis upon *coping* and what helped a child to cope, rather than upon the conditions that put children at risk. If our proposals were to concern the improving of preschool practice, then our research should have good practice as its focus.

A third decision followed from this. How to make manageable the question of how better to help children cope through exposure to good preschool practice? It is a broad question. We decided for several good reasons to focus upon one particular aspect of coping: what helps a child to concentrate or commit his attention in his 'work' and his play? We can consider some of the reasons for this decision later. There were many – practical and theoretical.

The seminar confirmed one final decision that proved crucial to our later operations – principally at the inspiration of our co-director Dr Harry Judge. Dissemination of knowledge about preschool education, our most experienced colleague believed, depends upon the existence of local networks through which knowledge travels out to the community of practitioners. If we wanted to observe the dissemination process as a system, we would do well to concentrate on a locale. We had from the start planned to stay local, to work on preschool provision and practice in Oxfordshire. The seminar confirmed it.

We were to study Oxfordshire at our doorstep. Any English county is a subtle amalgam of the local and cosmopolitan, of the statutory and the voluntary, of new and old social classes never quite at ease with each other, and in our county particularly, of town and gown. The nature of Oxfordshire as a county undoubtedly affected the results of our work. But there are universals in the particulars as well, and though we will couch many of our findings in local terms, the reader will, I hope, discern the generalities.

All counties, for example, balance their provision of preschool care between the voluntary sector and the statutory sector. In the case of Oxfordshire, the 36,000 under-fives were looked after in very considerable measure by voluntary playgroups, many of them set up and run by local groups loosely affiliated with the Pre-school Playgroups Association, a voluntary organization of which we shall have a good deal to say in later chapters. The PPA (and comparable groups) are to be found all over the United Kingdom playing much the same role. And our county, like every other, takes official cognizance of the under-fives by assigning statutory responsibility for them to both the Local Education Authority and the County Social Services. Statutory responsibility is quite clearly structured – the premises of any playgroup, for example, must be officially approved by a specialist worker from local Social Services. The operations of voluntary organizations, depending as they must upon the unpredictability inherent in the lives of young mother-volunteers, do not lend themselves to standard operating procedures. Wherever one looks, there is a marked gap between the outlook of the local government official and the volunteer. There may be conflict and there may be cooperation between the two – and there is usually both. But it is not a matter simply of personal whim or of good will and ill. It is built into the nature of the British system of caring for the under-fives away from home. But in other respects Oxford is particular. There are fewer working mothers than in many other counties. But we shall return to these matters in a later chapter.

Almost immediately the Project was proposed, the

buoyant hopes for preschool expansion that had brought it into being were deflated by the OPEC decision to double the price of crude oil. Britain's economic recession has worsened steadily since. The expansion of nursery facilities announced in Mrs Thatcher's *Framework for Expansion* had been premissed on an increase in financial support for education in general. Whether such an expansion would have occurred, even had good times continued, is a bit doubtful. Nothing in Budgets between 1968, when the Plowden Report first proposed expansion, and 1974, when OPEC sent crude oil to $11 the barrel, committed Governments of the day to an expansion of nursery education. Once the economic situation worsened, and once unemployment began to rise, hoped-for expansion turned into contraction. Yet up to 1974 Britain had increased its labour force principally by recruiting younger women (rather than, say, importing guest workers), and the need for nursery places had increased apace. In the decade and a half before 1974, while the increased proportion of working women was plainly evident, no substantial increase in public expenditure on the care of the under-fives occurred. In effect, then, our Project operated during a period not of expansion but of contraction – and a period of disappointment at that. One of the more vivid local dramas in Oxfordshire at the time our project was ending in 1978 was a sit-in to save one of the nursery schools in an industrial part of Oxford City.

A word, finally about how the book is organized. The chapter immediately following is concerned with the principal forms of preschool care available in Britain, how they came into being, how much they cost, what had been planned for them. This will serve as background for those unacquainted with the system. Chapter 3 sets the preschool scene in Oxfordshire and relates that scene to the country at large. Chapter 4 sets the research questions and policy issues in more precise terms. The next three chapters look in detail at the principal forms of preschool provision. These, in effect, are discussions of studies undertaken by several working parties in the Project – one on playgroups and nursery schools, a second on childminders, a third on full-day care centres. The principal findings of the first working party are in Chapter 5.*

Chapter 6 presents findings from the working party on childminding – the results of a survey of mothers, minders, and the children in their care.† The survey drew much on one carried out by Pat Petrie and Berry Mayall (1977) at the Thomas Coram Research Unit in London.

Oxfordshire, though it contains an industrial centre (Banbury) that employs young mothers in food processing, does not have extensive full-day nurseries. Minding serves instead. We were forced to go out of the county. Nine varied London day-care centres were studied in some depth by a small working party. They studied not only how children were looked after but how the establishments had been organized and how managed.‡ Their principal findings are reviewed in Chapter 7.

Although the working parties covered the main forms of preschool care available in Britain – playgroups, nursery schools and classes, day nurseries, and childminders – there was one further issue that needed to be explored – the involvement and participation of parents in preschool care. A considerable part of the initiative in founding and operating preschools comes from parents. Their role is likely to be even greater during the foreseeable period of economic pinch. A study of parent involvement in playgroups and nursery schools was undertaken by another working party. Unfortunately, the findings were not ready in time for inclusion in this book.§

As the Project was nearing its completion in early Spring

* A full account of this project is given in K. D. Sylva, C. Roy and M. Painter, *Childwatching at Playgroup and Preschool*, Grant McIntyre (1980); and in D. Wood, L. McMahon and Y. Cranstoun, *Working with Under Fives*, Grant McIntyre (forthcoming).

† See B. Bryant, M. Harris and D. Newton, *Children and Minders*, Grant McIntyre (1980).

‡ See C. Garland and S. White, *Children and Day Nurseries*, Grant McIntyre (1980).

§ T. Smith, *Parents' Preschool Involvement*, Grant McIntyre (forthcoming).

1978, Professor A. H. Halsey and I organized a seminar to reexamine what in fact had happened to past projects for improving preschool provision. There had been Plowden, the Thatcher *Framework*, the Educational Priority Area projects, American Head Start, and so forth. It was a varied and highly informative seminar. A good many very busy people came to help, and much was done towards recapturing policy perspective. Some of that perspective is contained in Chapter 8, the concluding chapter, which is concerned with policy for the future.

An Appendix, finally, looks in closer detail at one of our efforts to 'disseminate' knowledge by means of 'participatory research' with practitioners. It is a case study whose conclusions are problematic – for the issue of local dissemination remains problematic. It will perhaps give the reader a sense of the difficulties involved.

While this volume reports a good deal of the research of others in the Project, it is necessarily a personal and selective report. The conclusions set forth do not speak for all who have been associated in the work – though I have solicited their views and listened to them with respect. I have tried to write usefully for the general reader rather than the specialist alone, knowing that the other volumes emanating from the project contain fuller, more technical accounts. My concerns are with the general need for the provision of care for the under-fives, with how – in the present economic and social climate – more and better care may be provided, and with how it should be balanced. I shall review some of the major findings of the several studies undertaken and consider wherein different kinds of provision succeed and fall short, and how they may be strengthened.

Jerome Bruner

London
November, 1979

1

The search for policy

Childhood in the years before school begins is, by conventional standards, a family matter. We are repelled by the very idea of a national policy for infants and toddlers, for it smacks of invasion of privacy, or worse, of totalitarian efforts to shape young minds. It conjures up images of Chinese communes where children spend time each day packing little torch bulbs in wrappers in order to learn that they too are part of the labour that builds the State.

Yet every nation, implicitly or explicitly, has a policy towards its children. If it is pluralistic and *laissez-faire* as it has been idealized in the liberal ideology of the West, it is nonetheless a policy and it has its effects. It is a policy that changes slowly, but change it does and change it has done over the last century. It consists of many kinds of decisions: some have to do with 'safety net' provisions for children and families in poverty, in trouble, or otherwise at risk – the social services; others have to do with the provision of educational opportunity and the cultivation of human resources – the educational services. And these decisions can have, quite inadvertently, a strong impact on children and families. Taxation and tax deduction can favour the early education of children or penalize it. Delinquency can be defined punitively in legal provision, or in terms of remedial needs. Employment policy can make it possible for women to work part time in a way that makes child care possible or impossible. Housing estates can keep the needs of children in mind or create concrete nightmares. Every society defines in some way the uses it hopes to make of immaturity. It is inescapable. The only points at issue are *what* policy and *how* it should be arrived at. In most Western democracies, the decision process, the *how*, has classically tended towards indirectness, pluralism, and local control, in keeping with the democratic tradition. The 'policy' consists of a sum of small decisions, each option taken independently one of another, with occasional historic moments in which an effort at integration is made – often in the form of a White Paper. But increasingly in the last generation there has been a growing sense that, for all our devotion to local control and plural policy, children's lives are nonetheless deeply affected by events and policies that are national in scope and, so to speak, beyond the control of the families and communities who are by conventional assumptions supposed to be charged with bringing up a next generation.

The advantages of pluralistic and decentralized policy-making are, of course, obvious. In all its inefficiency, it provides for participation and involvement locally – closer to the grass roots where the effects of decisions are felt. But there are disadvantages as well. When social and economic change is rapid, needs often change faster than habits, and habit-bound local initiatives lag behind what later will be apparent as a crisis. I believe we are living through such a period today. The Great Depression and the war years – each sufficiently special to seem like historical exceptions – provided striking instances of national policies that profoundly affected the lives of children. Sometimes the policies consisted of a failure to take decisions or even to see that they were needed. Little was done, for example, during the Depression to buffer children from its devastating effects, though studies like Jahoda's of Marienthal (1971) warned that the children of unemployed workers suffered diminished aspiration and a deadening of fantasy that could be traced to living in the depressing circumstances of family unemployment. Unemployment simply has devastating effects on families and children, and unemployment levels in Britain are again very high, particularly among younger workers. There is evidence accruing that it may again be having a deep impact on family planning and family life in Britain (see for instance Sinfield, 1978). Not to respond to that fact once it is known is in effect to take a stand on policy.

During the Second World War, Britain's concern for the safety of children from bombardment led to their evacuation from danger areas to the country and to the establishment of nursery care for the young children of mothers working in essential industries. Never had there been such careful thought given to the out-of-home care of young children – both evacuees and the children of workers. A new spirit seemed to be stirring. Though there was agitation from the 'nursery movement' to continue some form of nursery care as a peacetime measure, the Government of the day held back and the wartime nurseries were simply allowed to fade away, as Tessa Blackstone so tellingly recounts (1971).

As cities have grown and the social order become more mobile and complex, there has developed a new awareness of the importance of public, national policies for the lives of children. The Socialist countries of Eastern Europe, for example, having decided that economic development required all women between 18 and 55 to work or study after their children were 18 months or two years, *had* to face the complicated technicalities of providing nursery care as part of redefining the new relation between family and community in the raising of children. It was never decreed in the democracies of Western Europe that women *must* work, but in fact they *have* entered the labour force in steadily increasing numbers for a half century now, and at a highly accelerated pace in the last twenty years since the end of the Second World War. As we shall see in the following chapter, Britain has been no exception to this growth. Who looks after the children of these working mothers, and how?

It is more than employment that has changed. Housing developments are an invariable feature of increasing urbanization. It takes little imagination (though some courage) to see that radical changes in habitat affect the lives of young children in a profound way – one only has to picture the young mother on the fourteenth storey watching her child being bullied by an older child on the playground far below. And with urbanization comes the scattering of the so-called extended family as well as of the neighbourhood – the aunts, cousins, and grandmothers and neighbours on whom a young mother could depend for support – or what is nowadays known more bureaucratically as 'support services'. The family, as a result, becomes more nuclear and isolated than ever. Nor is Britain apart from the world trend toward increased divorce and separation which many believe to be the result of the pressures and isolations of modern family life.

The more one examines the matter, the more evident it becomes that there is a far wider range of policy issues with 'child impact' than had been supposed. That phrase is itself a symptom of the times. It has been used as the title for a continuing public policy seminar, now in its third year in Washington, aimed at assessing steps that might be taken to reduce the negative effects of *all* government policy on childhood and human growth – in the spirit of the 'environmental impacts' statements required of new projects in America. But child impact is surely too negative an approach to the formulation of policies on behalf of families and children. During the run-up to the 1979 election in Britain, Mr Callaghan made much of his Party's concern for the maintenance of strong family life in Britain, though neither Labour nor the Conservatives have ever gone much beyond *expressing* their concern. A positive policy on behalf of children and families is urgently needed. Little question there is widespread feeling in the country that the time has come to take a more positive approach. Economics, chilling and compelling though the immediate prospects may be, does not justify risking a generation. Nor is it clear how expensive it would be to be wise. Britain has a lamentable record where the 'official' provision of care for preschool children is concerned. We shall examine that record in the chapter immediately following, but it is enough to say here that there has been a stolid lack of response to the stresses and demands of urban family life, particularly among young families with children under school age. What is curious about this lack of responsiveness at the governmental level is that it seems to be principally a carryover of ancient habits that have escaped the kind of re-examination that many social problems have in fact received in Britain since the War. There has been a long series of White Papers and legislative actions that have brought Britain to the forefront in social services and education during a period when, let it be noted, she was losing her overseas empire and shortening canvas in a series of formidable economic gales. Beginning with Beveridge and Butler and going through Court, social security, education, and social services were revamped to meet the contemporary conditions of a socially conscious, compassionate democracy. Yet there has been no comparable comprehensive examination of the plight of the family in Britain, and of young children before school-entering age. The Finer Report (1974) focused on the single-parent family; Court (1977) was principally about health and social services. Neither has provoked much by way of supporting legislation. Both political parties have at one time or another paid lip service to the need: the Plowden Report (1967) initiated by a Conservative Government and issued by a Labour Government and the Conservative Thatcher White Paper have intelligently and earnestly discussed the need for expansion in nursery facilities – and neither of these reports provoked much response beyond widespread press coverage. It is all the more curious in view of the fact that the two major parties might surely have recognized the degree to which political capital could be made of the issue of family and child care during a period when the electoral balance was on a razor's edge.

Could civil servants in the Departments of Health and Social Services and of Education and Science have failed to recognize that the new strains affecting families were arising not in the family itself nor in the local community, but in the broader social, economic and technological life of the nation – and perhaps of the world? The trend toward the employment of women, for instance, has been worldwide, and by 1977 about a quarter of British mothers of children under five were working full- or part-time. No serious effort has ever been made to assure, as an example, that fully-employed women might work two, three or four rather than five days a week, with job assured, so that they might take a hand in rota arrangements involving self-organized childcare groups. No effort has been made to provide tax deductions for employed mothers obliged to pay for the care of their young while they are at work. No effort has ever seriously been made until very recently to assure that facilities for child care related to working mothers are made in the construction of housing estates or blocks of flats. Instead, Britain has allowed itself to lurch from crisis to crisis, awareness at the public level flaring up only when such matters as child battering and the Maria Colwell issue, or the possible dangers of unsupervised child-minding or of 'latch-key' children, have made inaction both politically inexpedient and morally reprehensible.

Nor has the well-known contemporary phenomenon of clinical depression in the mothers of young children – first reported in the British clinical literature some years ago by George Brown and Tirril Harris – led to much other than the widespread prescription of tranquillizers by general practitioners to depressed and isolated young mothers. There seems to have been not so much a conspiracy of silence as an inert failure to recognize that something new is happening in British family life where mothers and children are concerned. And where social workers are involved – as with single parent families or with families under severe emotional stress – again there seems little provision made to cope with their reports and their statistics on the growing need for special care.

Nor have the trades unions shown any active appreciation of the problems, even the special one of the working mother. Only in the last few years has a Trades Union Congress working party reported on the inadequacy of the system of childminders and day nurseries and concluded (as we shall see in more detail later) that the system was grossly inadequate and ought to be re-examined 'root and branch'. In the main, however, none of the major trades unions, even ones with a sizeable proportion of women members, has been heard from. The National Union of Teachers, from whom reasonably one might have expected some response to the mounting difficulties of the preschool child and his family, has been principally concerned in fighting the battle for nursery schools and classes and their expansion, and for the security of teachers in such schools – very much a bread-and-butter issue, and not one looking to the broader public problem.

Even where there has been radical and successful action – in the private voluntary sector – little by way of 'support services' has been provided to make such voluntary efforts easier, more integrated or, more intelligently informed with modern knowledge about early childhood. I once asked a distinguished civil servant why so little financial aid had been given the Pre-school Playgroup Association, whose role in the establishment of voluntary preschool facilities has been outstanding and widely admired throughout Europe – and his reply was that they were so evanescent, so hard to pin down: 'It was even difficult to find out their address.' The inadvertent result has been that the PPA has grown into a vigorous, autonomous, locally controlled, and virtually unique self-help child-care movement. It would be wrong to give the impression that only the voluntary section has responded to need, or that local and central government either fail to respond or do so only in a ham-fisted or clumsy fashion. In fact, where the two have worked together effectively under the even handed leadership of a concerned local authority – as in Cheshire, to take one example – the results have been excellent.

The British are prone, in their way, to write it off, such a voluntary movement, as 'middle-class'. But that, in itself, deserves some comment in a discussion of national policy towards children and families. In 1972 and 1973, during the stewardship of Sir Keith Joseph at the Department of Health and Social Security, there was a lively round of debate and discussion led by the Minister himself, dealing with the special problems of children caught in 'the cycle of deprivation', children born into poverty and trouble who, it was feared, would then go on to become adults who would themselves raise children caught in the same cycle. The concept of social deprivation was then very much a part of public discussion and had come from America where it has been used by Patrick Moynihan to characterize poor Black families and by Oscar Lewis and others in discussion of Puerto Rican families who had come to urban America from the *barillos* of San Juan, importing their self-perpetuating habits of poverty with them. The concept of a cycle of deprivation has been widely criticized. Emphasis on the 'poverty-syndrome' either of the individual, the family, or the social group has been found to be exaggerated in such accounts and, in more recent years, more attention has been given to the broader social and economic forces that operate in a society to perpetuate poverty. The idea of compensating for deprivation by 'enrichment' has not stood the test of evidence. But all that aside, it was a period of genuine self-searching in Britain with respect to children and families suffering from inherited poverty. It was a pity that little came of the initiative in a practical way, for it came to an end with the defeat of the Conservative Government in early 1974. The Labour Government that followed tended to reject the whole idea on the grounds, not without basis, that the definition of the problem tended to place undue emphasis on the poor families themselves and not enough on the economy and the nature of the society which created them. In any event, they produced no comparable programme, and shortly after, the succession of shocks that followed the OPEC initiated oil crisis turned attention elsewhere.

One result of those discussions was that the problems of childhood and of young families was made to appear principally the result of poverty. Families above the so-called poverty line were seen as not having a particularly hard time. Theirs were 'middle-class' problems. In fact, the coping families, so to speak, are as we shall see having as hard a time as any, emotionally and socially. It surely makes little sense to sweep their problems under the rug on grounds that they are not in crisis or poverty. The task, it seems to me, is to assure that they stay out of crisis as much as they can possibly be helped to do so.

One last, but central issue should concern us before we turn to the details of present provision. It is the major concern of this book, though it cannot be treated in isolation from the broader issues of national policy with which we have begun the discussion. It concerns the nature and the quality of the care provided for preschool children away from home, be it in a playgroup, a nursery school, at a day-care centre, or at the childminder's. Indirectly, it is all about education in the broader sense. Directly, it is about the activities and the environments we arrange for young children when they are away from home. What should it be? Let me say only a word on this topic, for more will come up in the following chapter and after. The importance of early childhood for the intellectual, social and emotional growth of human beings is probably, as Lord Bullock once put it to me, one of the most revolutionary discoveries of modern times. Its critical significance still must be hemmed with some cautions, but let these not obscure the major fact: where emotional and mental growth are concerned, well begun is indeed half done. This is not to argue the point that bad starts are irreparable – for certainly Michael Rutter and his colleagues (1979) have demonstrated that even in secondary school, children who have been 'turned off' educationally can be turned on again by concerned teaching. But there is no denying the broader fact that the longer the neglect and the more established the child's alienation, the harder is it to bring him back to the process of education.

If this is true – and it would be folly in the face of two decades of research to gamble that it is not – then we must ask whether the preschool out-of-home-care for the child has kept pace with our knowledge of early human development. This is *not* to say that the object of the years before school is only to prepare the child for school any more than the years at school are only to ready him for work. The object of education at any age is surely broad and plural: to produce competent and zestful human beings who can manage their own lives and contribute to the common good whilst doing so. The lesson of the importance of *early* childhood is surely that we do all in our power to assure that the young get off to a healthy and competent start before they enter school. It would be comforting to conclude, therefore, that mothers should stay at home to look after their young. But if the conditions of modern life produce sufficient stress in young mothers to take a quarter of them to their practitioners with symptoms of depression and anxiety, surely this is not the full answer. Many mothers need relief from child rearing. Others wish to work or have to work. Obviously, mothers, whether they work or simply want their children to be away from home for part of the day, want the best care that can be had for them. Indeed, it is good for children (and good for many mothers of those children) to attend some form of preschool. In the main, they do better than others when given the opportunity. The issue is not *whether* there should be preschool provisions. They are here. The questions are, rather, what kind of preschool care, and whether we are ensuring that they are good enough to foster the healthiest growth possible. It follows, then, that every effort should be made nationally, locally, and individually to ensure that our practices in looking after preschool children are of the quality that can come only from careful planning and from the provision of advice and services that ensure excellence. Preschool practices that derive principally from conventional wisdom and once fashionable doctrines of child rearing are not good enough for a compassionate and concerned democracy coping with massive social change. It must be taken as a given in any national policy that the care of the young should be as thoughtful and considered as it can be made to be. Even if the principal activity of the years before school is play, there is play and play. Some of it leads to boredom, some to zestful curiosity. It would surely be dim to provide play for children without taking that into account. Whatever one's 'theory' of education, it must extend down to the preschool young. That does *not* mean educational heavy weather for the preschool child. It means only that we care about what we are doing and take thought about it – even if it is only the play of children.

Unless the broader issues of policy are taken into account, we shall fail to provide the best setting in which children can grow. *What* kind of provision, for what *purpose*, with what form of *responsibility*, for *whom* – these are the kinds of questions that must concern us, and to which we now turn.

2

Care away from home

In this chapter, we concern ourselves with the kinds of preschool care available in Britain, with the need for such care, with the amount and cost of care that is available, and with how these matters compare with expectations.

The kinds of care available

There are four major forms of care away from home available for under-fives, each with variants. Since there is a good deal of confusion about differences between them (even among the parents of under-fives), let me define each as officially understood, noting exceptions as we go. I will also try to give a sense of the clientele for each type of care arrangement. 'At home' arrangements – the baby-sitter who comes to the child's home and the live-in 'nanny' or *au pair* girl – are not included.

Consider first the part-time sector – institutions or groups that take children for part of the day and cannot, therefore, serve the needs of the working mother engaged in full-time employment.

The *playgroup* is, at minimum, a group of six children aged three to five looked after by some though rarely all the mothers of the children in attendance.* No matter how big the premises, a group rarely enrolls more than 24 children per session, chance and minor ailments then bringing the size to about 20. Typically, a session lasts for three hours, and if a playgroup has more than one in a day, separate groups of children and adults are in each. As the historian of the

---

* Chapter 3, on Oxfordshire, goes more specifically into playgroup arrangements – an easier task for a county than for Britain as a whole.

playgroup movement, Brenda Crowe (1973) puts it, 'all that can be taken for granted is that the premises and the playgroup leaders have been passed by the Social Services Department; that the ratio of adults to children has been fixed officially and, in some areas, that the groups have not been allowed to start unless the playgroup leader is "suitably qualified"'. In fact, the powers of the specialist workers in Social Services Departments is such that they can waive these requirements if they think it sensible to do so. They rarely do.

Playgroups were originally conceived as a form of 'do-it-yourself' nursery school and came into being in their modern form when in 1960 the Ministry of Education denied preferment in state nursery schools to the young children of school teachers. One of those thus deprived advertised in the *Guardian* for other parents who might be interested in setting up a cooperative group. From these informal arrangements has grown an enormous playgroup movement in Britain. As we shall see in more detail in the following chapters, the curriculum is not easily described and tends to focus more on play than on instruction.

From the start playgroups were set up to fulfil a variety of local needs, from combating the anonymity and isolation of high-rise flats, to encouraging hospitalized children, to 'mixing' in racially varied neighbourhoods. Whilst there are interesting experiments along these lines, the principal form of playgroup is a group of 'normal' children from a surrounding area come to play under supervision; it *is* rather middle-class in orientation, and is volunteer in structure. The biggest by far of the associations joining playgroups into a movement is the Pre-school Playgroups Association. It actively encourages its mothers to take a part in the operation of the group and, if they become decidedly involved in leading a group, to receive training in one of the courses organized by PPA tutors or by the local College of Further Education. The encouragement is subtle, ranging from the establishment of rotas to help in supervising the group, from facilitating children's participation in various group outings to help in various money-raising fêtes. A mother can, if interested, even go on after being a 'helper', if she chooses and has the talent, to do a tutor's course. There is a tacit understanding (in the PPA, if not among other groups, such as the Save the Children Fund) that volunteer mothers will shift to other matters when their own children outgrow the playgroup, and it is taken as a matter of faith that 'preschool parents' will go on to take an active part in parent-teachers associations later. In this sense, it is also a participatory movement for mothers. But it would be a mistake to overemphasize the central role of the PPA. It is highly decentralized and the local playgroup, while it may pay national dues, is most often highly autonomous and self-governing.

Some playgroups are in parents' houses but they mostly assemble in church halls or other public halls, often rent free, but sometimes for payment (at least in 1977) amounting to £1 to £2 an hour. They usually operate from 9.00 to 12.00 a.m., the afternoon being a less preferred time for a second group. Playgroup leaders who have qualified in a PPA course may get some pay after their group has been in being for a year or two, usually £1 or £2 for a three-hour session. Not all leaders take groups five days a week, nor do most children under four go each morning. The overwhelming majority of children are three and four, the occasional younger child or older one having slipped in for some special reason. The cost per child per three-hour session averages out to about 50p and some few pay nothing if need can be established.

Playgroups are run by what might be called qualified amateurs. The ambivalence of the movement toward professionalism is suggested by two quotations from Brenda Crowe (1973). Of leadership, she says (in her role as National Adviser to the PPA):

> It does not always follow that because a playgroup leader is an NNEB (Nursery Nurses Education Board) certificate holder, SRN (State Registered Nurse), In-

fant or Junior Teacher, or the holder of a degree, she is automatically better at working with three and four year olds and their mothers than someone untrained. Some good playgroups are run by mothers, or others, who had no training for anything after leaving school, or who had an apparently irrelevant training. However, it is already clear that *whether or not* playgroup leaders were previously qualified, they would be helped by a specially designed Playgroup Course.

And by the same token, PPA does not see itself as in the business of educating young children, but of simply providing a good opportunity for them to play with other children under supervision. Mrs Crowe, for example, contrasts 'good' playgroups with 'uncontrolled' ones at one extreme and 'rigid' ones at the other. Of the latter she says,

> These are more difficult to explain and understand, for the children often appear to be happy. . . . But play and child development are so little understood by many parents that they have no such clear idea of what constitutes being happy doing the 'right' thing, or happy doing the 'wrong' thing in a playgroup. In a rigid playgroup, the children's activities are often controlled in groups, and even timed by the clock . . .

As an association, PPA is trying to break out of what Tessa Blackstone (1971) calls the 'middle-class strand of child care', organizing mother and toddler groups, even considering all-day care on the semi-volunteer PPA pattern. That numerically it is a success story is attested to by the fact that since Belle Tutaev's letter to the *Guardian* in 1960 it had reached a half million children by 1977. The level of support for the playgroup movement varies considerably from region to region. Local support through County Education Departments varies widely, and amounts to some subsidization and support services in authorities like Cheshire and Inner London. In terms of grants given nationally to PPA from DHSS and DES, it has never exceeded a half million pounds in any year – somewhat less than £1 per child registered. Whether one regards these grants as generous or a pittance, it is the case that the chief source of energy and talent within the playgroup movement is volunteer, and such fees as it pays playleaders and supervisors are minimal. It has turned its voluntary status into a form of pride in accomplishment not unlike, say, the Royal National Lifeboat Institution where the pride is in the doing. Certainly the leaders, tutors, and regional advisers of the PPA generate an *esprit de corps* not unlike lifeboatmen!

Yet it would be wrong to give the impression that *all* playgroups have a strong participation by the parents of children in attendance, or even that *most* playgroups are directly run by parent committees. In most instances, notably in the case of PPA, some parents (a minority) are actively involved and interested. The remainder help in various ways for a day or so each half-term. But it is usually made clear in such playgroups that if mothers wish to help more, they will be welcome and, indeed, could receive training to do more. The 'boundary' between the volunteer playgroup and the parent is, so to speak, permeable and not defined by strict qualifications and professionalism. The boundary is somewhat less permeable in the case of playgroups run by such organizations as the Save the Children Fund, where the object is to provide a service. In the twelve thousand or so PPA groups, it would be fair to say that there is at least an implicit invitation to parents to take a hand in the operation, and in a later chapter on Oxfordshire we shall examine some of the ways in which this works out.

An obvious limitation of the playgroup as an institution is its part-time operation which makes it unsuitable for the care of children whose mothers work. In a large housing estate in Inner London, 'Parkview' (Andrews, 1979) there is a playgroup with 25 places; only four are taken up by residents of the estate. Other estate mothers with under-fives go off to work and must make other arrangements.

<u>Nursery schools</u>. If the playgroups are the lively newcomers on the preschool scene, nursery schools are the senior

service. They combine long traditions such as the kindergarten designed to stimulate the children of the more liberated middle-class, and the 'welfare' nursery school aimed at raising the working-class child from the conditions of the slum – Froebel, Pestalozzi, and Susan Isaacs on one side of 'self-realization'; Margaret and Rachel McMillan, Maria Montessori and Samuel Wilderspin on the side of 'help for the slum child'. There was never any question about the educational aims of the welfare nursery: it was frankly dedicated to improving the intellectual and practical and social skills of the slum child. In its middle-class version, there was likewise no question, until the advent of 'depth psychology', that the objective of the kindergarten was educational. The 'slum' school's educational objective was mixed with 'moral rescue', in which spirit Nancy Astor wrote her famous letter to *The Times* (of 18 August 1951) to say that it cost as much to send a boy to an 'approved school' for delinquents as it did to Eton. 'The problem of nursery school' she said 'should be gone into from a commonsense point of view.'

Perhaps Blackstone (1971) is correct in seeing the convergence of the middle-class and working-class strands in the emergence of the 'developmental' idea – the idea that the preschool is neither to *give* an elementary education nor to *prepare* for one, but to help *develop* the 'natural child'. Saving the would-be delinquent from the ravages of his broken home or the middle-class child from excessive adult pressure – these now could be seen in a common perspective.

All of which provides a good introduction to the nursery school in contemporary Britain. For in general it tends to be strongly concerned with creativity and expression, and has been until recently very resistant to seeing its function as 'pretraining for school'. The shortage of places for rising-fives in infant schools and the new emphasis upon the importance of early linguistic and intellectual skills has begun to change that. But there is much expressed concern for the individuality and expressiveness of each child. The children in attendance are three to five and in Oxfordshire they average around 40 per school. A nursery school, typically, will have two or more teachers and an NNEB qualified nurse. Teachers are almost invariably trained in nursery education at a college of education or polytechnic, or as infant-school teachers specializing in 'young primary children', and are employed full-time. Their working day usually starts before the starting hour of 9.00 a.m. and extends an hour beyond closing time around 3.00 or 3.30 p.m. Teachers also report spending a fair amount of time talking with parents about children's (and parents') problems, and their calling may often be emotionally demanding. Not all observational studies of nurseries agree on this point, however, and Barbara Tizard reports that such 'consultation' is rather rare. Nursery teachers are among the lowest paid in the teaching profession. Nursery schools are state schools and there are no fees for attendance (though there are also some few private nursery schools that charge up to £1,000 or more per year for a four-year-old.)

The nursery schools of a county, as State institutions, typically have a working contact with and get support from the Advisory Service of the Local Education Authority, and the liveliness of the exchange depends upon the interest of the Local Education Authority and the keenness of the nursery teachers.

As with playgroups, nursery schools do not provide a solution for the working mother. At Tower Hamlets in 1979, for example, there was a long waiting list for places in the day nursery, but vacancies in nursery school places.

It is not easy to characterize *nursery classes*, save by contrast with nursery schools. Nursery schools are free standing and not part of other institutions. Nursery classes, also for the three to fives, are usually physically and administratively part of the Infant Primary schools. Like nursery schools, they are State schools, charging no fees to those enrolled. In Oxfordshire, there is an average of 30 children per nursery class. Unlike the nursery school, directed by a Head Teacher who is likely to be very clearly in charge, nursery classes are in the charge of the Head of the Infant and Primary School and taught by teachers trained usually in the teaching of lower primary school classes. The curriculum varies, and in later chapters we shall encounter some of the differences as met in Oxfordshire. Like nursery schools, nursery classes have access to the advisory and training opportunities provided by the County Education Department. Perhaps it could be said of nursery classes that they are more school-like than nursery school, but it is not strikingly so.

Specialist child workers in a county's Social Services often place problem children in nursery schools and classes but this is always with the consent of the Head. It may become a source of some tension and dissatisfaction when the number of such children becomes large enough to be felt by teachers to be disruptive.

Nursery teachers (from nursery schools and classes) are joined together in the British Association for Early Childhood Education (BAECE), which has county branches. Very few belong to the more politically active NUT. The world of nursery school teachers is middle-class, joined by a personal network, based on tacit assumptions about childhood and its cultivation. Perhaps the sharpest contrast between the playgroup and the nursery school is in parental participation, which is usually much less in the latter than the former.

Consider now the services available for children who need to be looked after for a longer part of the day than covered by nursery schools or classes or playgroups.

Childminders. Technically, a childminder is any person who looks after other people's children between the ages of zero and five, and does so for monetary reward. A mother (or father) typically brings the child to the minder's before work in the morning and picks him up again at the end of the working day – which will vary of course with parents' hours of employment. There is very wide variation in what the child will do at the childminder's. In some instances, he will do little other than tag along as a spectator member of the household. There have been instances of children remaining idle and passive through the day with really nothing to do. Other childminders take the children in their care for excursions or, indeed, take them to a playgroup for a morning session. It is very difficult to generalize about the national picture. Obviously the care will vary with the facilities, outlook, and background of the minder.

The typical minder is herself a mother looking after her own as well as others' children. In Oxfordshire, for example, the 480 registered minders each were authorized to look after two children besides their own under-fives. The minder typically does her own housework while minding her charges. What is unique about the service is that a working mother can leave her child when she needs to in the morning, and pick him up when she is free again at the end of the day.

Minders may or may not be registered with the local authorities. It is uncertain how many minders there are in Britain, for not only are many unregistered, but there is also a fairly rapid turnover among the registered minders, who may or may not stay long at the job after registering. A minder must, in registering, have her premises approved as suitable, and there are safety and space standards applied by local social service departments. In most counties and boroughs in Britain, there is no particular incentive for a minder to register: she receives little benefit in opportunities for insurance rates, and only very rarely in terms of support services. Sanctions are not applied against the unregistered minder. The major benefit for the minder is being on a social worker's list who may then pass her name on to mothers in search of a minder's services. Some training schemes have now been organized for minders by local authorities and two London boroughs are experimenting with schemes to pay minders on a regular basis, collecting fees directly from parents. These plans are meant as incentives to improve the facility of minding and to encourage registration.

The historical roots of childminding go back over a century. Childminding was originally associated with the expansion of the great Lancashire spinning mills in the nineteenth century, but its social history has not been closely examined. As we shall see later in the chapter, there is a continuing shortage of state *maintained* full-time places for the care of the young children of working mothers. There has, accordingly, been a steady increase in demand for minders, who have provided the accordion pleat to accommodate a growing need.

Full-day nurseries. A day nursery is a well-housed, professionally staffed 'home away from home' where children can be left by a parent before work and picked up at the end of the day. The activities almost always include conventional nursery school or playgroup activities with clay, paints, water and the like for older children, and the nursery routine with cots available for the children for naps and rest. The children play far more in group settings than they do at home, but aside from that it is difficult to characterize the atmosphere of day nurseries, for they vary as widely as views of caring for children in groups vary. They also vary widely in size, most caring for between 20 and 40 children, with staffs varying widely from two or three to eight or nine. Some take children as young as eight months, but more usually they begin at age two or even three.

There are full State maintained day nurseries, plus those run by charitable or community organizations, and also some run by commercial organizations. Some full-day nurseries have also been set up by women working at such institutions as universities, colleges, and hospitals. Some few have been established as crèches by factories with large numbers of women employees. Maintained day nurseries used to be run (as was all day care) by Local Authority health departments up to 1970, since when they have come under the jurisdiction of local Social Services Departments. A study of Lambeth, Manchester, and Leicester reports that social service workers there regard provision of day care as 'preventative social work, and not as a service provided for all in need' (Community Relations Council, 1975, p. 14). And this view prevails in other boroughs and counties. Priority for the places in day nurseries is usually given to children 'at

risk' – those whose parents have marital or psychiatric problems or who are at risk in other ways. Priority is also
provided for children of single-parent families. Day nurseries
are not envisaged as a service for the children of working
mothers. Such children are admitted mainly to 'keep the
balance'. As already noted, places in nurseries are in short
supply. Getting an ordinary child a place at a day nursery
usually means a long wait on the list. In Lambeth, for
example, where the provision of places in maintained day
nurseries exceeded fourfold the DHSS guideline of 8 per
1,000, the borough could provide for only half of its *priority*
children.

Mixed models. There has been a move in recent years to
set up combined centres that locate a full-day nursery and a
part-day nursery school in the same premises, and as of
mid-1979 there were about two dozen of these in England.
They enrich the day of the nursery child, although they
create certain staff tensions between nursery nurses on the
day nursery side and teachers on the school side, who
operate on different pay scales and holidays, and have somewhat conflicting views of their roles. There is considerable
interest in such a model from the point of view of providing a
more comprehensive service, but the costs are of course
high.

Yet another model that is emerging is the extended day
playgroup in which parent participation is more prominent.
There has been some discussion of such extended day
playgroups in the PPA, although no policy decision has been
taken about them. We will encounter one in a later chapter
when London day nurseries are under discussion.

Again, childminding and day nurseries have occasionally
been used in alternative ways. In Edinburgh, for example,
application for a place in a State day nursery may be accepted
and the child temporarily or indefinitely assigned to a minder
paid for by Social Services in the event that no day nursery
places are available. Social workers report that such assign-
ment often leads to dissatisfaction in the parent who feels her
child is getting 'second best'.

The need for care away from home

How much need is there for various kinds of preschool provision in Britain? Can it be sensibly assessed when there is so wide a divergence of views about what constitutes 'need'? The topic, alas, lends itself to polarization. The humane view is that every family has the right to as much 'reasonable' care as they deem necessary. But 'reasonable' is not easy to define. Does it include the right of mothers to work while their children are young? Should it take into account the nature of the setting – city versus country? Who shall bear the costs? In times of rapid and uncertain social change, occurring in the midst of economic stringency, little is served by dogmatism on such issues. The facts of modern family life in Great Britain raise all manner of problems for which we have no ready-made answers. We might properly begin by considering some of the factors that have increased demand for preschool provision. Among them are (a) the number of women working, (b) the increase in single-parent families, (c) the scattering of the extended family and the attendant pressures on the nuclear family, (d) the new status of women, (e) the stress and isolation of urban family living, (f) the changing philosophies of childhood, and (g) the reappraisal of the influence of infancy and childhood.

Take first the issue of mothers at work. The increase in Britain's labour force in the last quarter century is made up almost entirely by the entry of women into employment. In 1951, there were 15·6 million men employed in Britain. In 1976 that figure was 15·9 million. In 1951, there were 7·0 million women at work, in 1976 10·0 million. The male labour force has increased by 2 per cent in a quarter of a century, the female by 43 per cent (CSO *Social Trends*, 1977, Table 5.2). If we now ask who are these women who have swelled the British labour force the answer, unequivocally, is that they are married women. The figures are striking. In 1951 there were 4·3 million unmarried women at work, since which time that number has declined steadily until it had reached 3·2 million in 1976 – a net loss of 26 per cent. The number of married women employed in 1951 was 2·7 million and that has risen steadily since to 6·7 million in 1976, an increase in the married female labour force of 148 per cent! If we probe still further into which sector of the female married population has contributed most to the work force, it turns out to be married women with children, and if we take the 1960s as the period to examine, we find that in that decade, the percentage increase in employment for mothers of the under-fives was the highest of all – 63 per cent in the decade. What produced the change, of course, was the earlier age of marriage and, with it, the earlier age at which women began bearing children. But whatever the cause, the fact is that Britain over the last decade and a half has witnessed a huge increase in the number of married women at work who have small children.

More specifically, there were 19 per cent of mothers of under-fives in the labour force in 1971 – part- and full-time (*Census 1971: Summary Tables*, 1 Per Cent Sample, Table 37). This adds up to about 590,000 women. By 1974 the figure had increased to 26 per cent, some 900,000 young mothers at work, of whom about 185,000 were working full-time (Bone, 1977). The authoritative Report of the Central Policy Review Staff of the Cabinet Office, issued in 1978 (*Services for Young Children with Working Mothers*) estimated that there were 900,000 young children in Britain with working mothers: 700,000 whose mothers worked less than 30 hours a week, 200,000 with full-time working mothers. By international standards, the figure is not high. Swedish figures indicate more than half of mothers with children under five at work. In any case, high or not, there is a very large number of children in Britain today who, because their mothers are at work, need care away from home for part or all of the working day.

What leads women to work? It is obviously some mix of necessity and choice. Poor immigrant women with children under five work because they have to make ends meet. In Leicester in 1971, 85 per cent of 'coloured' mothers of under-fives were at work, 71 per cent in Manchester, 44 per cent in Bradford, and so forth (Relations Community Council, 1975, p. 9). And when in 1974 a cross section of mothers of under-fives was asked whether they preferred to work, more than half who were in families with an unemployed head and living on less than £20 a week said they did. The comparable figure for mothers in families earning more than £60 a week was 20 per cent – a sharp reduction by contrast, but still a considerable figure (Bone, 1977). For mothers of the under-fives in general (leaving out those who were single-parents and the sole support of their families), virtually three in ten want to work. Of the single-parent mothers, the figure is close to three quarters.

It would be a serious error to interpret the increase in women at work as the result entirely of economic pressures. Indeed, at the lower end of the scale, the pressures are ferocious and the figures cited for coloured immigrant women can only be interpreted in that light. But many young mothers wish to work, and the reasons often lie beyond economics.

One predisposing factor is the condition of life in modern urban society: anonymous, technical, and mobile. The extended family of traditional society no longer provides a supporting net, and its successor, the modern nuclear family, often isolates mother and child from close relationships with others. A sense of helplessness develops. A major conclusion of last year's Report of the Carnegie Commission of Children (Kenniston, 1977) surely cannot be true only of the United States. It says:

> If parents are frustrated, it is no wonder: for although they have the responsibility for their children's lives, they hardly ever have the voice, the authority, or the power to make others listen to them.

In Britain a recent Government survey (Bone, 1977) indicates that about one third of parents of preschool children have been unable to find the out-of-home help they feel they need in raising their young. Whereas the traditional extended family included aunts, uncles, and grandparents who might share in child care, the result of displacement into an urban area is to cut off effective links with close kin (Stacey, 1960). The urban setting provides little by way of community. A recently completed survey of a high-density inner-London housing estate included interviews with the tenants. The most pronounced dissatisfaction was found among the parents of young children, regardless of playground facilities nearby or the height of their flat. The same study indicates that in this London housing estate, neighbourliness is 'casual and involuntary' and there is very little visiting. Those who are most disorganized by such circumstances of living are unable even to take advantage of playgroups and other facilities laid on for parents with small children (Shinman, 1975). Not very surprising, then, that there is a considerable incidence of disturbance that has aroused the concern of psychiatrists. A study by Brown (1978) estimates that 25 per cent of the mothers of children under five are at one time or another on tranquillizers for depression and allied disorders. A comparable epidemiological study in Oxfordshire yields a very similar figure (Skegg, Doll and Perry, 1977). The conclusion that seems to emerge from all this is that many young mothers are eager to find some means of getting either relief from the chores of child care by part-time arrangements – playgroups or nursery schools – or by taking jobs that bring them into contact with other adults for a good portion of the day.

There is one special psychological spinoff that affects *urban* family life. The city is a dangerous place for children – however exciting it may be. Mothers in cities feel less capable of coping with their children and their problems than they do in the village or rural setting. Perhaps the most comprehensive study to date on this problem is by Graves (1969). She compared rural and urban Spanish Americans around Denver, Colorado, rural and urban Buganda, and around Entebbe and Kampala in Uganda. Her interviews reveal that urban mothers come to believe more than their rural sisters that their preschool children cannot understand, cannot be taught ideas or skills by them, cannot be depended upon. The city mother rates her preschool child less independent, less self-reliant, and less helpful with family matters than does the country or village mother. It is not inconceivable, although we cannot know, that the irritability and frustration of urban mothers both produces the behaviour in children of which mothers complain and produces the perception of them as less capable and worthy. The urban environment seems both to restrict the child and harass the mother.

There have also been ideological changes that have affected the definition of family responsibility. The historian Edward Shorter (1976) argues that the trend in family life from the nineteenth to the twentieth century is from 'community obligations' to 'self-fulfilment', from 'allegiance' to 'sanctioned egoism'. He writes:

> Market capitalism was at the root of the revolution in sentiment . . . . The logic of the market-place positively demands individualism: the system will succeed only if each participant ruthlessly pursues his self-interest, buying cheap, selling dear, and enhancing his own interests at the cost of his competitors . . . . Thus, the free market engraves upon all who are caught up in it the attitude: 'Look out for number one.'

Shorter sees the isolated nuclear family not just as a result of the geography of industrial urbanization, but as a psychological matter as well. In the mid-nineteenth century, the 'liberated woman' was concerned to nurture the family, free of the pressure of work. Prosperity and the new technology turned women inward to their families – created a *more* nuclear family. But with the evolving of market capitalism, Shorter proposes, the nuclear family became the battlefield of a new civil war with women finally looking for outlets *outside* the family in order to fulfil *their* aspirations for individuality. What is certainly evident is that some very fundamental changes have been and are in process and they are altering the pattern of modern family life. Whether 'market capitalism' is the root cause must remain moot, for the changes in progress seem to be as profound in Britain as in America, in Holland as in Hungary, in Egypt as in Japan. And how much such socio-cultural factors interact with the Pill as an instrument in family planning, under the control of the woman, is very difficult to assess. It is said to reduce the size of families. Does voluntary choice also affect commitment to families already in being? Divorce is strikingly on the increase. In the United States, divorce affects more than one marriage in three, and Britain is moving toward that figure. In absolute terms, there has been an increase in divorces made final from 29,000 in 1951 to 79,000 in 1971 to 120,000 in 1975 – a quadrupling in a quarter of a century. Indeed, from the point of view of families with children under five, divorces have increased from 18,000 in 1970 to 33,400 in 1975. This partly reflects changes in the laws governing divorce, but those changes themselves reflect the altered situation.

A recent survey by Harmon (1977) in the United States noted that the number of children under six living with single parents had jumped 'by a staggering 54 per cent' between 1960 and 1973, 'such that by 1974 over 15 per cent of all under-six children were living in one parent circumstances'. While in 1974 in the United States 62 per cent of single mothers worked, the figure for all married mothers was only 40 per cent. But more striking still, the children of single mothers were far less fortunate economically. They *had* to work.

> . . . while 8·7 per cent of children living in families headed by men were doing so at income levels lower than the officially determined poverty level, 51·5 per cent of those children in single-mother-headed families were in that condition.

The figures for Britain are comparable. In 1971, 3 per cent of two-parent families were on supplementary benefits, but 46 per cent of the fatherless families (Finer, 1974).

While more than half the nation's 24,000 maintained day-nursery places were filled by children from one-parent families, the provision of places was so meagre, however, that only five in one hundred children under five in one-parent families were looked after. This figure is far below any standard figure on need formulated in the White Papers of the sixties and seventies. It is ironic that in the ten-year development plans submitted to the Department of Health in 1962, only five local health authorities had plans to expand their day nurseries – and this at the start of a decade in which the British divorce rate was to treble and the female labour force to increase dramatically (Blackstone, 1971).

Nor has it been easy for the single-parent mother to wend her way through the bureaucracy to obtain help for reimbursing childminders and baby-sitters while she works. A case was *sub judice* before the Inland Revenue Special Commissioners in 1978 in which a divorced working mother who was the single source of support of her two children was appealing her right to deduct expenses for childminders and baby-sitter as 'necessarily' as well as 'wholly and exclusively' for the performance of her job. A previous ruling, Halstead v. Condon, had found that it was not deductible. The ruling has been sustained.

Less tangible changes are affecting the demand for pre-school care – ones that do not lend themselves to close statistical analyses, but which are nonetheless important. Two of these are particularly important: the changing status of women and the changing conception of childhood, both products of the last quarter century.

The first is the 'women's movement'. It has affected not only sexual politics but the politics of domesticity. Women insist more upon autonomy. They are plainly not as prepared to be isolated as much as before while bringing up small children. And as the role of physical strength in work is replaced by technical qualifications, job opportunities become available to them. So women have been doing better in 'men's' subjects and their performance in Britain on O and A levels has improved faster than their male fellow students'. As young mothers, they are often more qualified to get jobs than their mothers would have been. Being 'just a housewife' has even become a phrase of slight opprobrium.

Changing conceptions of childhood have also affected the demand for preschool provision. There has been increasing emphasis in recent years on the importance of an *early* start for the child in the preschool. It is now generally accepted in the community that the early years matter in later development to a degree not before envisaged – matter socially, emotionally, and intellectually. The roots of this belief are nourished both by new research and old historical movements.

There is, to begin with, an increasing conviction that children very early in life should get used to other children and learn to get on with them. In Turner's recent study of playgroups in Ulster (1977), this was given as the principal reason for sending children to playgroups and it is a reason usually near the top of the list for sending children to nursery schools or playgroups. It may well be a reflection of the anonymity of urban society, of the absence of cousins and easily accessible neighbours where the isolated nuclear family has succeeded the more connected extended one. What before happened naturally must now be arranged. It may be an accompaniment of the 'other orientated' society of which Riesman (1950) wrote so persuasively two decades ago. The insistence that the preschool child 'learn to get on with his peers', whatever its origins, has certainly increased demand for preschool provision.

Doubtless too, the widespread (and principally middle-class) belief that the family by itself can generate a scenario that may stifle the child's spontaneous growth contributes a share to the demand for early preschooling. Freud and common sense 'depth psychology' have probably popularized the idea that for some part of the day it is good to 'get the adult off the child's back'. The fact of the more isolated nuclear family must surely have reinforced this belief. It took me rather by surprise to see how many brochures of nursery schools in Greater London commented on the importance of allowing the child to be free part of the day from 'adult pressures'. Interestingly, it was not until the studies of Brown and Harris (1978) on depression among young mothers that there was much public talk about the importance of 'getting the child off the mother's back'.

A new reason for preschool experience came on the scene in the 1960s. Research in America had shown that an early drab environment depressed intellectual growth. This was very quickly generalized in popular accounts to a concept of 'cultural deprivation' and projects were mounted in America and in Britain to 'compensate' for such initial deprivation. Indeed, there was a period in the mid-1960s when the more intellectual Sunday press in America and Britain produced a spate of articles on the importance of early stimulation in general. That publicity may have added to the demand for more preschool facilities.

In summary then, the demand for preschool care has increased not only for hard economic reasons, but for subtle and psychological ones as well. It is difficult to know on the basis of what has been said how much need there is for that kind of care. This is particularly true of the relation between full-day care and part-day care. It is sometimes predicted that there will be a decline in economic activity over the coming decade in Britain, in which case there may well be a sharp decline in female employment. But this is anything but certain. It is highly unlikely that there will be a decline either in the number of single-parent families where the mother must work or in the inflation fuelled economic squeeze that leads married mothers to go out to work to supplement family income. Where part-day care is concerned, all of the indicators point to a continuing increase in demand – and certainly the mushrooming of the playgroup movement speaks to that absolute issue. True, the decline in the birth rate will reduce the size of the under-five population. But the proportion of children in that population whose parents will be wanting preschool provisions for their children will doubtless rise.

The provision of care: promise and performance

The history of child care in Britain since the war is a curious counterpoint of unfulfilled official declarations of intent, and voluntary response filling gaps left by inaction. In 1978, Britain had one of the poorest child care records in Western Europe in the maintained sector, and arguably the best record in the world in the do-it-yourself care of the under-fives.

First with respect to implied promises. Contemporary targets go back at least to the Plowden Report of early 1967 and were reiterated in Mrs Thatcher's 1972 White Paper, *Education: a Framework for Expansion*. The latter acknowledges the targets of the former in the following passage (Paragraphs 16–17, pages 4–5):

> The Plowden Council estimated that provision for 90 per cent of four-year-olds and 50 per cent of three-year-olds would be adequate to meet the demand. The action the Government now propose will give effect to these recommendations. Their aim is that, within the next ten years, nursery education should become available without charge, within the limits of demand estimated by Plowden, to those children of three and four whose parents wish them to benefit from it.

The actual recommendations of Plowden are contained in the following table drawn from the Report (Table 10, page 128, Vol.1).

Age	Time	Percentage of group	Full-time equivalent places needed 1975	1979
3–4	Full	15	132,900	137,400
3–4	Part	35	155,050	160,300
4–5	Full	15	130,800	136,650
4–5	Part	75	327,000	341,625
		Total	745,750	775,975

Table 1.1 *Nursery Education: Number of full-time equivalent places needed (where part-time defined as half-time)*

The cost (in 1975 money) of the projected plan would

have been roughly as follows. The White Paper recommended that 'most' of the expansion should take the form of added nursery classes, without specifying what the fraction should be. We may take the ratio of 2 to 1, nursery classes to nursery school as an appropriate guess. This would mean the provision of 500,000 full-time nursery class places and 245,700 nursery school places. On average for that year, a full-time nursery school place cost £482 per annum, a place in a nursery class £305. The total cost by this reckoning would have been £272 million per year. This does not include money for building costs, and the decline in the birth rate might have provided much of the space needed. However reached it is a great deal of money for part-day preschool provision.

In fact, of course, the provision of care has fallen far short of those figures. A fair estimate from the Association of County Councils is the following (ACC, 1977).

	Time	Nursery Schools	Nursery Classes	Total
Threes	Full	6,023	12,398	18,421
	Part	20,398	47,629	68,027
Fours	Full	8,062	137,096	145,158
	Part	12,808	61,181	73,989
Rising fives	Full	588	171,188	171,776
	Part	622	7,193	7,815
Total children		48,501	436,685	485,186
Total full places		31,587	378,683	410,270

Table 1.2 *Actual provision of nursery school and class places*

In 1975, then, there were only 55 per cent of the children envisaged in the Plowden quotas actually in attendance in nursery schools or classes. In a word, half the under-fives in Britain were without a place in maintained preschools. And among the under-fours, the figure is more like one in ten of those envisaged by Plowden. What took up the shortfall between promise and performance?

The answer is playgroups. As we have already noted, the playgroup movement begins in the early sixties. By 1970, the number of children catered for was 170,000. By 1977, to put it in the bare language of *Social Trends* (CSO, 1977).

> The Preschool Playgroups Association estimate for England and Wales a membership of approximately 11,000 groups in April 1977, and the number of children on register was over 400,000. In Scotland, at 31 March 1976, there were approximately 1,800 playgroups catering for about 49,500 children.

Close to half a million children.

Since playgroups and nursery school serve the same set of family needs – provision of part-time care – we should examine their relative costs and performance. Costs certainly are quite different: the cost per child in nursery school is £475 per year at 1975–6 prices. The comparable cost for a child at a playgroup is, using the same 1975–6 base, £140. The difference undoubtedly reflects the costs of professionalism and the savings from volunteer helpers as well as shorter hours in the playgroup. Nursery schools and classes are conducted by qualified professionals in the ordinary sense of that word: people with diplomas from sanctioned courses, and other formal qualifications. They operate in costly premises. The non-volunteers who go through the training scheme of the PPA receive a small stipend. The moot question is, then, which can Britain afford and what in the long run are the benefits to be derived from the one form or the other. The PPA, being designed to attract mothers into helping as a matter both of principle and economic expediency, may have a spin-off in community building and the creation of a sense of self-sufficiency. Although many preschool professionals would reject the idea of comparing the 'performance' of the two forms, one careful study indicates that playgroups do as well in encouraging language skills, social-emotional growth, and general intellectual development (Turner, 1977). The improvements found in that study were comparable to those found in earlier studies of nursery schools. But one study, in Ulster, however carefully done, does not decide the issue. The real question, I think, is which form of preschool can best do what, and how much each can be improved – issues to be revisited in later chapters.

British women in voluntary association have by their own efforts, then, gone a way toward making up the shortfall between the implied promises of the 1972 White Paper and the need for care. Roughly half of those envisaged by the Plowden and Thatcher reports were attending nursery schools and classes, in 1975. Those quotas may have been low. A report by Bone (1977) reports that a third of the parents of under-fives feel they are not able to find the preschool provision for their children that they believe they need. The record gives no cause for complacency when compared with Britain's EEC partners. France, with perhaps the most generous system of child allowances in Europe, does far better than Britain at providing care away from home: 25 per cent of two-year-olds, 70 per cent of three-year-olds, and virtually all fours attend state financed preschool facilities. Many of them open from 8 a.m. to 6.30 p.m. to cater for working mothers.

Turn to full-day care. The British maintained system deals meagrely with the working mother and her problems as we already know. The bare facts are these. In 1978, there were 200,000 full-time working mothers with children under five (CPRS, 1978). Fewer than a fifth of their children were provided for by maintained nurseries or crèches. The number of places has changed little since 1961 as the following figures show (*Social Trends*, CSO, 1977, Table 3.5).

1961	22,000
1973	24,000
1974	25,000
1975	26,000

This covers a period when, as we know, the number of women in the labour force increased by a couple of million and the number at work full-time by tens of thousands. And since many places are assigned to children whose families are in difficulty, the figures do not really speak directly to the issue of full-time working women.

No surprise then that most of those who wish to or must work avail themselves of other means. The most available means is childminding. One cannot determine the number of childminders in Britain and the number of places they provide. An unknown number do not register. Some indication of the growth of minding can be got from the lists of those who do register. In 1961, minders provided places for an estimated 14,000 children. By 1973 that figure had risen to 92,000, since when, with increased unemployment and declining births it has fallen to 85,000 in 1976 (*Social Trends*, CSO, Table 3.5). The OPCS sample survey of 1974 indicates that about three per cent of children under five are cared for some of the time by childminders. About one child in ten who is getting away-from-home care is going to a childminder (Bone, 1977, Table 2.7). There is, by the way, little difference in this proportion as one moves up and down the social-class scale. Childminders, we may note, are preferred principally for the care of younger children. A third of mothers wanting care for their children during the first year prefer them, but the figure drops to two in a hundred by the time their children reach four.

Putting the matter in gross summary terms where full-day care is concerned, the figures for 1976 were roughly 30,500 children in day nurseries, and 90,000 with minders, accounting for only 120,500 of the 200,000 under-fives whose mothers were full-time members of the labour force (CPRS, 1978). As with playgroups and nursery schools and classes, so too in full day care the private, more improvised arrangement has outstripped the official, statutory one as far as numbers are concerned. We cannot even account for where many of the children go when their mothers work!

What can be said about the comparative costs and merits of day nurseries and childminders? No surprise that the cost of a day nursery is strikingly higher than the cost of a minder:

approximately £1,000 per child per year for a day nursery place, and £280 with a minder – both at 1975–6 prices. Day nurseries may simply be too expensive in their present form for the public purse unless they can be shown to provide a unique service. How good are day nurseries? How good is childminding? Can they be made better? We shall turn to those issues in later chapters.

The conclusion that has suggested itself to many observers of the British preschool scene is reinforced by our closer analysis of trends and figures: the principal provision for the under-fives in Britain is *informal* or *voluntary*, dependent upon the efforts and labours of non-professionals, housed either in private dwellings or structures designed for uses other than the care of children away from home. Britain may be on its way toward becoming a socialist state in other respects, but in the crucial respect of child care it is far from it. Neither in times of plenty (the 1960s) nor most certainly in times of scarcity (post-1974) has there been any indication of major support for preschool care from the State – in spite of high levels of promise from governments of the day, Labour and Conservative alike. But throughout this period of 'benign neglect' there has been ceaseless activity in the forging of voluntary organizations to look after part-time care, or of private initiative in providing full-day care. For all the effort, it should be repeated that, as a government survey shows (Bone, 1977), a third of the mothers of under-fives in Britain are still unable to find the help they feel they need outside the home in raising their children.

3

The setting: Oxfordshire 1975–8*

As a preparation for looking at the quality of care available in Oxfordshire, we look at it first as a microcosm. Is it typical? What are its problems? How is care delivered?

The old county of Oxfordshire was independent of Oxford City. Each had a self-sufficient Education Authority and Social Service Department. They were joined in 1974 as a new county (encompassing as well the northern part of old Berkshire) with a combined population of 535,500, 118,500 residing in Oxford City. There are two sizeable towns outside Oxford, Abingdon (21,000) and Banbury (35,000), each based upon light manufacturing. The county is, thus, a mix of intensive and on the whole prosperous farming and of manufacturing, the chief focus of which is on the edge of Oxford where the Cowley works of British Leyland employ 15,000 workers. But it is not polarized between concentrated industry and intensive agriculture. There are a fair number of small towns which, like Banbury and Abingdon contain light industry – Witney, Wantage, Wallingford, Bicester, Chipping Norton, and so on.

The County Council's Research and Intelligence Unit estimated in 1976 that there were 38,197 children under five in the County. The size of each age cohort varying roughly between 6,000 and 8,000 children, the larger cohorts being the older children, for Oxford's population reflects the national decline in birth rate.

As a county, the new Oxfordshire resembles a large cluster of other non-metropolitan counties, suburban metropolitan districts, and outer London boroughs with respect to

* A great deal of the sifting of documents and interviewing that went into the making of this chapter was done by Mrs Miriam Harris.

social indicators such as numbers of working mothers, economically inactive late-teenagers, unemployed, unskilled, large families, minimally educated, etc. Its 'next-of-kin' counties are Bedfordshire, Gloucestershire, Cheshire, Kent, Leicestershire and it is like such boroughs and metropolitan districts as Croydon, Hillingdon, Stockport, and Solihull. It is statistically at about dead centre. On the list of 23 social indicators used by the DHSS (Imber, 1977) for judging counties and districts Oxfordshire is neither in the top ten nor the bottom ten of the 108 places on eighteen of these. On two of the indicators, it scores high: car ownership and pensioners living alone, the highest on the former, and among the lowest in the latter. Not surprisingly, Oxfordshire has a high proportion of 'economically inactive males' for that is the category into which students are put. Economically, the county is rather well off; it ranks 25 in 108 in rate of unemployment.

With respect to indicators related to the under-fives, the county is somewhat above average (it ranks 34 in 108) in proportion of population aged 0–4, close to the middle in terms of a crowding index for housing (57 in 108), right at the middle in balance of home ownership and rental tenancy, and somewhat favoured in having fewer single-parent families (83 in 108). On only one index, and a very relevant one, it is quite markedly extreme. It has the smallest proportion of full-time working mothers with children under five of any county or metropolitan district in England – 17·4 per cent in comparison to 56 per cent for the London Borough of Haringey, 52·6 for Brent, or 51·9 for Ealing. A plausible reason for this is that the principal industry in the county – cars and their components – is not a big employer of women. And although industry might have been expected to attract immigrants, the county is near average in both New Commonwealth and Irish immigrants.

If, finally, we take Oxfordshire's average rank on the 23 diagnostic social indicators used by DHSS, it ranks about sixtieth in the 108 counties, boroughs, and metropolitan areas. Its only distinction relevant to our study is the small proportion of young mothers who work full time. Places for their children should not be in short supply.

Recall that there were, during the years of the study, roughly 38,000 under-fives in the county. If we examine the facilities available for them in preschool care we do indeed come out with a not unfavourable picture (using for comparison the national figures outlined in Chapter 2). Nursery schools and classes and playgroups provide nearly 7,000 places.

	Places
Nursery schools and classes	1,148 part-time
	380 full-time
Playgroups	5,280 part-time
Total	6,808

Table 3.1 *Nursery school, class and playgroup provision in Oxfordshire*

Reckoning roughly 7,500 children per age cohort, the county has places for some 45 per cent of its threes and fours. More than three quarters of these places are available by virtue of the existence of a strong playgroup movement in the county which has established some 291 separate playgroups varying in site from industrial areas such as Cowley St John to rural villages in the Vale of the White Horse.

The provision of full-day care for full-time working mothers is less favourable. The percentage of mothers of under-fives in the county working full time is 17·4 per cent (Imber, 1977). Assume conservatively that each such working mother has one child. Taking the county total of 38,197 children, this yields an estimate of 6,644 under-fives in need of full-day care. There were three local authority full-day nurseries in the county and another eight that were privately run, totally 311 places. That is a tiny proportion of the places needed. Add the 522 registered childminders with places for 1,327 children – a figure whose validity is hard to judge since many registered minders no longer mind. Since registered minders have been increasing in number, let us assume they provide 1,800 full-day places at registered childminders and at day-care centres. This means that slightly more than a quarter of the children of working mothers are being 'officially' provided for. The remainder must be either in the care of relatives or of unregistered minders, the proportion of each of which we are unable to estimate. Compared, perhaps, to inner London this may be 'good', but in any absolute sense, it is not much of a provision. There is a shortfall of close to 75 per cent in the provision of registered places in a county with the smallest proportion of full-time working mothers in England. In the final analysis, of course, the significance of the shortfall rests upon the difference in the quality of registered and unregistered minders. In fact, the difference may not be so great (cf. Chapter 6).

The Education Department of the county is unexceptional, sympathetic to early childhood education but neither strongly fighting to maintain or increase its financial support during the period of shrinking grants in 1976–8 nor coming out strongly for economy. Oxfordshire, like most counties, has a staff of educational advisers for first and primary schools and *their* responsibility includes nursery schools and classes too (and, in a rather unspecified way, also playgroups). But of the eight advisers only a half of one's time is concerned directly with nurseries. The Senior Adviser has stood for the maintenance and expansion of nursery education with no ambiguity whatsoever, but beyond his direct influence, the advisers have little contact with preschools. They occasionally visit nursery schools (as they may also do playgroups) to discuss pre-reading and pre-mathematics curricula or to help put preschools in contact with schools where children will next enroll. The involvement as far as supervising staff was concerned is inevitably quite minimal because of short staff. There are after all 14 nursery schools, 14 nursery classes, and over 250 playgroups. Educational influence or directives from top down are not much in evidence. Indeed, there is little time or inclination to regard the variety of preschools as a system or as a whole, and policy towards them is non-existent or piecemeal.

Many of the teachers in nursery schools and classes are members of BAECE – the British Association for Early

Childhood Education. BAECE does have some influence through meetings and workshops and the Chief Adviser has cooperated with them on the presentation of topics as varied as reading, maths, and school entry.

During our study, the nursery world in the county was much beset by cuts and threats of cuts. They were not in a venturesome or exploratory mood. Many were suspicious of playgroups as a sellout of the nursery ideal. Indeed, some nursery school heads were concerned that our Project might be comparing their form of provision with playgroups, providing ammunition to the anti-nursery forces in the Education Department.

Playgroups in the county are indeed a success story – the 250 or so cater for more than 5,000 children – virtually all are affiliated with PPA and all have been set up within a decade. For all that, PPA organization has always been loose, was always *intended* to be loose. Lady Phelps–Brown, the County President when we started, expressed concern in our first conversation that the Association might become too hierarchical, too organized, too ridden by requirements. Local playgroups get three things from central PPA – two material, one 'spiritual'. The former are bulk buying of play materials and PPA courses. The spiritual gain comes from being part of a movement actively and successfully concerned with the care of children – including one's *own* children. There are a dozen or two women who give greatly of their time and energy at the county level. For the rest, loyalty and focus is on the local playgroup – but the Association matters to them as well: Annual General Meetings of the County PPA are well attended. Short of that, I think PPA also expresses an aspect of the woman's movement, specialized for young mothers.

What of 'official control' of playgroups? County Social Services are charged with their oversight as well as of childminders and daycare centres. The department is, like the LEA, broadly sympathetic to the needs of the preschool child in the county, but their resources are much more limited. The LEA commands about 70 per cent of the county's budget (of which only a tiny part, to be sure, goes for preschool provision); Social Services 11 per cent. Since that percentage covers all age groups in the community, Social Services is thin on the ground where the under-fives are concerned. The county is divided into eight areas with a social services team for each area. But in the whole county, there were only four specialist workers whose particular training was with children, and only one of these was full-time. By the end of the project all the areas had some part-time provision of this kind. They concentrate on registering childminders. Such intermittent contacts as they have with playgroups relate to health and safety standards. Only Oxford City had a full-time specialist worker; elsewhere the 'child-task' was handled as a part-time job, sometimes as little as one day a week, and sometimes as part of the rather full case loads of regular social workers. The net result is that, save in respect of health and safety, Social Services has little impact on either playgroups or on childminders.

It was not clear what relation existed between social workers, primary advisers and specialist workers where playgroups were concerned. All specialist workers were given a broad brief to encourage playgroups. Indeed, the LEA even made funds available to Social Services to be allocated by the specialist workers for starting such groups. Advisers, on the other hand, saw no particular role for the specialist workers (one of them described their function as 'being responsible for counting the loos'), although one specialist worker was a trained nursery school teacher and another experienced in playgroup work. Nonetheless, a grant for aiding playgroups came *from* the LEA *to* Social Services amounting to £13,000 per year for 1975. It was a one-shot grant. While this averages little more than £40 per group it suggests that Education was not eager to get more deeply into playgroups on its own. Small though grants were, they were a considerable source of encouragement and gave starting-up groups a sense of being 'recognized'. In the main, however, the social worker was more often seen as an opponent in the endless process of trying to meet regulations for playgroup premises. And the approval of premises from the point of view of space and safety seems to be their principal job.

PPA's style and mode of organization is crucial to their success. Each local playgroup is truly 'the centre'. Even the published national organization plan inverts the usual pyramid and features 'your playgroup' at the top, the machinery of advisors, tutors and committees feeding into it. Each affiliated playgroup pays quite moderate annual dues to the National PPA, a fraction then being passed on to the county and branch organization. After the retirement of Lady Phelps-Brown from the county chairmanship midway through our study, her duties were divided among no less than three co-chairmen – one in charge of finances, a second to keep contact with national and regional offices, and a third (Avril Holmes, who also worked part-time with our Project) in charge of training and information. The county itself is decentralized into eight branches, each with an area organizer who acts as adviser, convener of meetings, and organizer of field days, coffee mornings, and other means for raising modest funds for expenses or 'scholarships' for 'needy children'. County PPA typically runs courses (sometimes with local colleges of further education) for playgroup leaders or for training tutors. It is a considerable network, highly decentralized and sparked by part-time volunteers.

In view of their importance for under-five provision, we asked Dr Judy Bradley to conduct a sample survey in the county in 1976. She looked in detail at 20 playgroups. The oldest dated back to 1963, but the majority came to the scene from 1969 onwards. All of them have thrived, the average group catering for 18 children at their start and now averaging 42, morning and afternoon sessions combined. Most of them cater for three to fives, with a few exceptions going younger or cutting off at four. Half of them have five morning sessions a week, most of the remainder four, a few only three. More than half of them have a group in the afternoon as well, although in most instances two or three times a week rather than every weekday. Fees per session vary slightly, but virtually all were charging between 30 and 40p per session in 1976 and all raise funds on their own through the usual mix of jumble sales, stalls at local fêtes, coffee mornings, and open days and all gladly receive gifts and donations from friends. All but three received grants from local authorities ranging from £20 to £145, but clustering around £50 per year.

All but one are administered by a committee of parents including the playgroup leaders, the exception being one run by a local community association in which parents are also active. Eighteen of the 20 groups came into being when mothers clubbed together locally and decided to start one. The other two are traceable to the individual initiative of a particular mother, starting a group around her own children and recruiting other mothers. Nineteen of the 20 groups are affiliated with PPA (none with any other association), but in effect they are on their own. Only one playgroup reported frequent visits either from social workers or from PPA advisers, though many of the groups are in touch with head teachers of local schools. When we asked whether they would like to have more contact with advisers or social workers, most said they didn't feel much of a need. All the PPA affiliates reported receiving and looking at the official publication, *Contact*.

The playgroups are situated wherever they have found space: a dozen in church halls, another half dozen in other public facilities ranging from a sports pavilion to an old school. Only one had facilities for transporting children (other than volunteer vehicles for outings) so the catchments were strictly local. Premises were rented at what might be called derisory fees, a few at even less. The average rent came to a bit over £1 per session. Amount of rent paid and excellence of facilities bore no relation whatsoever! Some of the best facilities came rent free.

Most supervisors were trained – principally in PPA courses, some as teachers or as nursery nurses. So too their helpers: six in ten had either PPA training or had done some form of professional work with children before coming on to the group. There was an average of four paid staff per group – though supervisors rarely received more than £2.50 per session and their more regular assistants rarely more than £1.50. Most usually, rota helpers were unpaid volunteers and the route to an assistant's or supervisor's role was principally through a PPA training course, which all groups encouraged. Parents, fathers and mothers alike, played a part in fundraising, committee work, outings, maintaining equipment. As Dr Bradley put it, 'Without parents providing help both in sessions and back-up support, many of the groups would clearly cease to function.' She went on to say, 'Parental participation in sessions was highest in the poorer areas, and appeared to be of as much benefit to the mothers as it was to their children. It enabled them to meet together in a social situation as well as providing them mutual support in the care of their children.'

But autonomy has its costs. Most of the groups were isolated one from another, even when they were in adjacent neighbourhoods. Only a few seemed interested in turning to other groups for ideas or practices. Orientation and loyalty were inward to one's own local group. As an exercise in local community building, playgroups are plainly exemplary. The 'failing' grows from that very strength: there is only a slow trickle of information and innovation from the centre outward.

So much for part-time provision in the county. What of full-day care – childminders? They are the responsibility of Social Services, a body that we have already described as thin on the ground.

Responsibility for childminders falls to the so-called specialist workers who register and check up on minders (though we shall see in a later chapter that this rarely happens). Registration goes as follows. Inquiries come from potential minders, and the list of applicants is long, as a result of the shortage of specialist workers. The intending minder is sent guidance notes spelling out her legal responsibilities in some detail. It is then up to her to follow up her application. If she does, a specialist worker will call, see the premises and interview her. At this stage, everything will depend upon that specialist worker's impression. If she is satisfied, she will leave a form to be filled out. If she has any doubt, she will not, for once a form is made out it is very hard to stop its processing. The operative legislation on the registration process is vague – health, safety of the environment, and criminal record being the triad of criteria mentioned to us. If an applicant is refused, she can appeal. So unsuccessful applicants are excluded informally by not being left an application form. If further doubts develop, the specialist worker has other ways of delaying – sending fire inspectors, insisting on X-rays, and the like. It is hard to know how 'conscious' this screening process is. It is not one that women find inviting, particularly since the benefits they stand to gain are rather negligible (see Chapter 2). Many minders, it would be fair to say, couldn't care less whether they are registered or not. It would be equally fair to say that the policy for registering minders is vaguely conceived, uncertainly executed, and quite mindless of the psychological needs of children.

As for a support system for minders in the county, there is little indeed. They are rarely visited after registration. They can, if they wish, get a small grant to attend a course at the local College of Further Education, but these are the courses designed for playgroup leaders. There are a few brave 'little' efforts at support that have failed. A sum of £500 was set aside by Social Services for 'toy libraries'. The specialist workers (recall three of the four were part-time) were given £100 each. The aim was rather unclear. Were the toys a diagnostic instrument for gauging how minders play with children, or were they to be toys on loan to minders? Our own interviews with minders (Chapter 6) found no trace of the plan having reached them though some active minders in Abingdon and Didcot did try them out. It would be not far from the truth to say that there was no support system available to minders.

A final word about Social Services and minders. The effect of being short handed overall is to make Social Services

increasingly crisis minded. Childminding is not a crisis problem. It mostly relates to mothers who wish to work, and
rarely involves them directly with social workers. Making it
possible for mothers to go to work is not seen by Social
Services as one of their main tasks, if their task at all. There
may even be some opposition – though not official. We
heard the sentiment expressed that a decision to work should
not be made 'too easy' to take. Altogether, we were struck
in interviews at how little the issues of women's employment
or women's changing role entered the discussion of child
minding or of the need for a supply of good childminders.
There was certainly little sign of awareness of the recruit-
ment of millions of women into the labour force in the last
fifteen years. Perhaps this reflects Oxfordshire's
bottom-of-the-league standing on woman's employment.

The day nurseries in the county seemed not to be much at
the centre of anybody's attention. They were, of course,
supervised by Social Services. The three local authority
nurseries (in Oxford and Banbury) are seen principally as
meeting needs of one-parent families under stress. They
were routinely visited by social workers. The two in Oxford
were housed in war-time, hut-like buildings, both with play
space around them, divided into large rooms where children
are formed into large groups rather than the usually preferred, smaller 'family groups'. The admissions policy was to
restrict them to children over a year but not over three, at
which age they are sent to nursery schools (and because of
Social Services sponsorship, they invariably are accepted and
their supervision shifted to the Education Department).
There are no links between the two full-day care
systems – minders and nurseries.

The picture that emerges from this brief account of
preschool provision is not an encouraging one – the only
highlights are the playgroup movement and, possibly, the
emergence of childminders to meet local needs. Certainly the
statutory part of the picture, in particular where support
systems and supervision are concerned, is dismal. In spite of
good will in both Social Services and the Education Depart-

ment, neither resources nor staff have been available to do much.

There is a dreadful irony in this. For in fact, Oxford had had great expectations, and the account I have set forth is a tale of how those expectations (save the playgroup movement) were defeated by circumstances.

Prompted by Mrs Thatcher's 1972 White Paper, *Education: a Framework for Expansion*, and the 1974 reorganization, there was established in Oxfordshire in 1974 a Working Party under the joint chairmanship of the Director of Social Services and the Chief Education Officer. It included eight members representing those two Departments plus one to be nominated by PPA. Its brief was:

> To review the provision in New Oxfordshire of pre-school facilities for children 0–5 (day nurseries, daily minding, playgroups, nursery schooling, etc.) including –
>
> (a) The present extent of facilities and the current arrangements.
> (b) The identification of principles on which services are presently based, and those on which they might in future be developed.
> (c) Suggesting ways in which future administrative arrangements and professional development can best be organized bearing in mind the interaction of educational, social service and voluntary responsibilities and interests.

Eighteen months later it produced a report, 'Beginnings'. It is a highly intelligent, humane, and well-informed report. It bears strongly the stamp of John Coe, the Senior Adviser for Primary Education. By the time it was completed, Britain's economic climate had worsened drastically. Not only could its proposals not be implemented; its spirit was destroyed. It was a plan for building and there was to be none. 'Beginnings' survives more as a symbolic charter than as a working document. It recognizes the centrality of early childhood in human development, points to the needs of children for challenge and stimulation, grants the over-whelming evidence on the importance of early learning for later intellectual development and of the importance for the child of opportunities outside the home, emphasizes the crucial role of affection and attachment for the child's security, faces up to the risks to families that have parents who themselves had unsuccessful childhoods, and shows a notable sensitivity to such non-child matters as housing and employment in affecting the state of families. It comes out firmly for an expansion of nursery schooling, opts for childminding over full-day nursery centres, urges the conso-lidation of administrative control for the different kinds of services, sets forth plans for coordinating the activities of playgroups and urges that they form closer links with min-ders. More PPA training and ten playgroup advisers are recommended. Indeed, in the section on childminding, there is one of the rare public admissions from a county body that working mothers represent a special problem – though the wish to work is presented in the canonical form of their being required to do so by the worsening economic situation.

By 1976 the Education Department had been forced to retreat to the point of issuing a small do-it-yourself pamphlet for parents, enjoining them to be mindful of their under-fives as real people, to converse with them, and in general to recognize that child is father to man. A county that a few years before had forged plans for an integrated provision of services for the under-fives was, by 1978, fragmented, under-staffed, without a working policy, without fall-back plans. There was a nursery sit-in to protest closure, there was bitter debate, there was suspicion in the nursery school sector that playgroups would replace them as an economy measure. The statutory sector, even had there been plans for the future, was so understaffed that they could scarcely do their job of registering childminders and playgroup sites, far less give leadership. That, of course, is what unfulfilled promises create. And that is the Oxfordshire in which our study was set. It was not much different from other places.

4

A closer look at the under-fives

In the three chapters that follow we look through the microscopes of particular research studies at what goes on in preschools, at the minders, and in day nurseries. The details are not always encouraging, and indeed, at times they provide some cause for deep concern. But before plunging into the world of the under-fives and their 'care givers', it might be worth a moment to describe what gave shape to the research projects that will concern us.

We had not contemplated a comparative study of the three basic forms of care: the part-time playgroups and schools, the childminder, and the full-day nursery. Each meets different needs in the community. Part-time preschools serve principally two functions: the first is to prepare the young child to cope with the world outside the home which includes getting him ready for the world of school. The second, however much it may remain implicit, is to provide mothers with some time free of the pressures of small children at home. Childminders serve a quite different function. They are, perforce, virtually the only resource available to the working mother. By any standards there are far too few day nurseries to take care of the children of these mothers. Indeed there are too few even for the mothers who must work to survive. Day nurseries as presently instituted serve principally the function of looking after children who are at risk – many of them from single parent families or families in trouble or need of some other kind. That is a challenging function, made the more so by the handful of children of working mothers who manage to get in.

The three research projects cannot simply compare whether a playgroup is better than a day nursery or a nursery school better than a minder. Each study, rather, focuses on tasks central to the different provisions. In the immediately following chapter, for example, we examine whether and how part-time preschools do in fact prepare the child for the world beyond the home, including school. Do they give the child an opportunity to master his ability to concentrate, to elaborate his play constructively, to engage in extended conversational exchange? Is he free, happy and undistracted enough to do these things? And is he self-disciplined enough to take advantage of his opportunities? Do playgroups, nursery schools, and nursery classes make all this possible and are there sensible proposals possible for improving the job they do?

Childminders are supposed to provide what some would call a 'home away from home'. Do they succeed? How do children compare in terms of their ordinary conduct at the childminder's and at home? That is the question that parents ask (and childminders do as well) and it is the question that was central to the agenda of the Sunningdale conference of 1976, called by the Government to discuss this form of care.

Day nurseries pose a still different problem. Obviously they too must ready the child for life outside the home – but they must also in many instances shield them from a disturbed home. The child at a day nursery spends a day away from home that is far longer than he will ever spend at school for years after. Some few are principally for the children of working or student mothers. Others are principally for referred children judged to be at risk, with the 'ordinary' child given a place if there are any left over. Still others serve special functions, such as providing immigrant children with language skills or even with survival skills for living in an alien culture. The full-day organization of any day nursery, whatever its function, is formidable. Our approach to day nurseries, consequently, focused more on organization than did either of the other research studies undertaken. How does a day nursery go about being a therapeutic community? How does it help children of immigrants master survival skills? What are the special problems of looking after the children while their mothers are being educated at a university? Can full-day care be delivered as a 'product' of commercial firms? Can they grow out of the voluntary efforts of playgroup-like enterprises? These are some of the practical questions that must concern us when we turn to day nurseries.

There is surely a virtue in uniform procedures for comparing different forms of provision for the under-fives – and it would have been highly desirable to incorporate comparable measures of child behaviour in each study. But research, alas, is short. Our grant was for three years. So it was our deliberate decision to look at each form of provision in terms of whether *each* was fulfilling *its* function. But at the end we shall also have to make as intelligent a surmise as we can about how the different provisions can be combined, what they can learn from each other, and so on.

The study of part time provision in nursery schools and classes and in playgroups was conducted principally by the use of a carefully designed observational schedule for studying what children did at preschool – particularly how they elaborated their play, interacted with other children and staff, and (above all) what they actually *did*. An auxiliary study was carried out on teachers and play leaders in preschools to help them observe their own behaviour with children as they might better achieve their *own* intentions in teaching or playing with children. The study of childminders was conducted principally through detailed interviewing of mothers, of the minders with whom they left their children, supplemented by observations of the children interacting with their mothers and with their minders. All of this work was done in Oxfordshire. The study of London day nurseries had two foci: one on the behaviour of children staying through the day and how they got on with each other and with staff; the other on how the day nursery had come into being, how organized, and how staffed. The account of our venture in 'dissemination through collaboration' is one man's image of what happened when the Oxford Preschool Research Group tried to form a working alliance with the child-care community of Oxfordshire. Whereas the first three studies can lay claim to some generality, in that Oxfordshire and London can lay claim to a certain representativeness, the account of our effort at collaboration is rather different. It is about the problems of bringing together research and practice in a local community. For any local community is unique, and perhaps therein lies its universality.

There are few more passionate topics in the family life of Great Britain today than the adequacy of care for the under-fives. It is as much a constant topic of neighbourhood talk as it is a taboo one in the high councils of government, whichever party is in power. I have, in the Chapters 5 to 7 following, tried to report as dispassionately as possible the results and conclusions of the three studies undertaken in our preschool project. That done, I shall try to look at provisions now available with a view to whether they are sufficient, whether they fulfil needs, whether they operate in the light of available knowledge, and whether they add up to an adequate national policy towards the under-fives. Finally, an appendix deals with an effort to disseminate our findings in a collaborative venture.

I have already confessed my doubts as to whether there now exists in Britain anything like an adequate policy toward children. The present patchwork of local arrangements reflects poorly the spirit of a compassionate society. The chapters that follow will recount some of the bases for my doubts. But it will also set forth some of the achievements of the curiously mixed system of British preschool provision out of which, I believe, most of the needed improvements can be fashioned.

5

Schools, classes, and groups

This chapter is about children who go to nursery schools, to nursery classes, and to playgroups – what they do there, how they fare in different kinds of activities, how they get on with those who look after them or who seek to instruct them. We shall, in the final section, also be concerned with how the ones who look after children in such preschools interpret their jobs and what they feel they are trying to accomplish in working with children.

The reader will have sensed in earlier chapters that the terrain on which we now embark is rather surprisingly riven by conflicts. What is the 'right emphasis' in such preschools? How shall children be treated: how much, for example, should they be 'instructed' and how much 'let free' to develop their own creative spontaneity? There are many slogans and exhortations. But curiously enough, rather little is actually known about what really happens in the preschools that children attend – whatever type they profess to be. It is less surprising that there are differences in point of view for, after all, the philosophy that motivates practice in a preschool is a reflection of views about the nature of childhood and, in a deeper sense, of convictions about 'the uses of immaturity' in the making of adults.

Part of our initial task was to explore the present state of provision for the under-fives and, as already related in Chapter 1, we early decided to explore at first hand the various kinds of part time provision available – including nursery schools and classes organized within the public sector, and less formal playgroups organized by volunteers. Part of this task was undertaken jointly with practitioners in these institutions, and some of the results of that joint enterprise will be up for discussion. But one of our professed aims was also to conduct a straightforward study of children in preschools in Oxfordshire – much as one might carry out a field study of children anywhere.

Our advantage, of course, is that an enormous amount has been learned about observing children in natural settings in the last decades – partly, ironically enough, thanks to the pioneering work of the field ethologists who have taught us so much about how to observe creatures of any species, bird, ape, or man. The investigation was carried out by a special task force in the Project – in charge Dr Kathy Sylva, a trained psychologist who had indeed done her doctoral thesis some years before on children's play; Mrs Marjorie Painter, who joined us on leave from her duties as head of nursery education at the Lady Spencer Churchill College; and Carolyn Roy, a research student with particular skills in the study of children's language. For convenience and brevity in referring to their study, we shall call it SRP, and the reader may get the full account from their forthcoming book.*

How observations were made

The bare bones of the study are easily described – though the observation schedule used and the statistical analysis employed in drawing conclusions need to be studied with care for a full appreciation of their data. They decided for good reason to use an observational procedure that is often referred to as the 'target child method' (described briefly in Chapter 4). What it amounts to in studying the behaviour of children in groups (or, for that matter, deer in a herd) is that rather than trying to characterize what the group as a whole is doing (an impossibly daunting task) one concentrates upon a single child as target and attempts to get a comprehensive account of *his* or *her* activities over a set period of time. In the case of SRP, the child's activities were noted during each

---

* K. D. Sylva, C. Roy and M. Painter, *Childwatching at Playgroup and Nursery School*, Grant McIntyre (1980).

half minute in a manner to be related below, observation carrying on for 20 minutes. In fact, each child observed was revisited some days or weeks after, and another set of observations was made for another 20 minutes. One hundred and twenty children were observed in this fashion, each for two twenty-minute periods. Roughly half were three-and-a-half to four-and-a-half, the other half four-and-a-half to five-and-a-half. Half were boys, half girls. And the three types of preschools were roughly evenly represented: nursery schools, nursery classes, and play groups. In gross time, this amounted to 4,800 minutes of observation – 80 hours or roughly 30 days of the active life of children in a preschool.

It is demanding work, and the observer has to keep her eyes open. During each thirty-second period entries must be made on a code sheet: 9,600 entries in all for the study. An entry addresses itself to 12 different matters in the child's activity during that half minute: what his task is, what it is part of, what his social situation is with other children or adults, with whom he is talking and whether it is connected dialogue or a one-shot remark, and so forth.* So twelve decisions at each of 9,600 entries yields 115,200 decisions to be made about individual children in groups. Arduous though it may seem, the method is the only guarantee we have against the bias that so easily intrudes when one sets down an overall impression, however artful. In fact, the observers *did* put down their impressions after each twenty-minute bout, though only as an aid in interpreting the more detailed data. It was this exercise in observation, as noted in Chapter 1, that teachers in training found to be such an eye-opener.

Since SRP is available to those interested in the full account, I want to gloss over the details of method and analysis,

* The decisions are (1) immediate task or activity (2) larger 'bout' of which immediate task is part (3) cognitive complexity of task (4) cognitive complexity of larger bout (5) how many others present (6) is child interacting with others or parallel to them (7) status of others (8) if adult is present, is her role active or passive (9) is another activity embedded in or parallel to the main task (10) how many utterances spoken (11) are utterances connected or 'one-off' (12) who initiates utterances.

describing them only in connection with the findings that need reporting here. But there are a few general points about method that help in elucidating a great many different specific results, so let me explain these first. As noted, the child's task (or lack thereof) is entered on the observation schedule for every thirty-second block. But obviously, tasks are started before any particular thirty-second period and spill over into periods following. These longer-lasting activities – be they pretend play, art work, pushing a toy car around – are commonly referred to as 'bouts', a clumsy though conventional name that we might just as well stick with. We can, then, speak of 'bout length' to refer to how long a child went on with an identifiable activity and even, at the extremes, talk about individual children as 'concentrators' and 'flitters' according to their typical bout lengths.

But it is also possible to stay within the thirty-second periods and ask some telling questions about how they are filled. We can ask how much talking went on (and in connection with what sort of task) and whether it was connected talk or 'one shot'. And by the same means we can tot up time spent alone and time spent interacting with others, and who the others were – children or adults. The method also makes it possible (by computer extraction afterwards, of course) to discover what kinds of social interaction in what kinds of activities characterize long or short rounds of play. Another more subtle matter comes within reach of the method as well. The observer can, it turns out, make a quite reliable judgement about the 'level' of the activity: how elaborated it is in the sense of involving component or constituent activities to realize a theme, or achieve a goal. This one can judge much as one can the complexity of a sentence by its dependent clauses and references backwards to what has been previously said, or forwards to what is about to be said. It is better, I think, to consider level of activity in conjunction with particular kinds of tasks, and I will return to it then.

No method of observing, obviously, is *the* perfect one. The one used in SRP has the virtue that it requires only common sense description rather than 'deep' interpretations of what is going on. That is what makes it 'reliable', a word that means simply, in this context, that several observers watching the same behaviour can agree about what has happened. It does not demand judgements of a child's security or anxiety or feeling of spontaneity. And while this may be a shortcoming, it is what one might call a principled shortcoming in the sense that highly interpretive judgements made by observers are notoriously unreliable. It is virtually impossible, in practice, to interpret whether a child is feeling secure or being spontaneous. Such interpretations are better made of an entire record on which one has rated what the child is doing. And it *is* indeed possible to penetrate to such deeper levels by careful inference from the records of the SRP procedure. What does one make, for example, of a child who is principally solo, flits from task to task, none of them much elaborated, rarely talks to others and never to other children? It may not be possible to categorize him in a diagnostic pigeonhole, but it certainly is possible to say that he is not getting involved in comparison with other children in the group.

In any case, shortcomings though it may have (and as any other method would also have), the method yields some extraordinarily interesting and, at points, counter-intuitive findings about children operating in preschool groups. For a start, I would like to concentrate (admittedly in too Olympian a manner, perhaps!) on what one finds in *general*, and without regard to whether the children in question are in nursery schools, nursery classes, or playgroups. For there are certain 'universals' characterizing children in groups that want consideration before we turn to differences observed as one moves from one kind of group to the next.

Activity with challenge

The first question – and it should indeed be the first in an inquiry of this sort – is: What is it that challenges children in preschools? What is it that produces rich play and engages the children's fullest capacities? What tasks, what social situations bring out their best?

SRP are quite clear on this point. The richest activities in terms of complex activity evoked almost invariably have two characteristics. In the first place, they have a clear *goal* and some *means* (not always obvious) available for its attainment. And secondly, they almost always have what for lack of a better name can be called 'real-world feedback' – the child most often knows how he is doing, whether it is building, drawing, or doing puzzles without advice from another. He may seek praise or approval. But he knows his progress on his own. These are the 'high yield' activities. Somewhat behind them are play involving pretending, play with small-scale toys, and manipulating sand or dough. And well behind these come informal and impromptu games, gross motor play, and unstructured social playing about and 'horsing around'. These rarely lead to high-level elaboration of play. Much of the latter unelaborated play appears to be serving the function of release of tension – in physical activity or in sheer social contact and 'chatting'.

Elaboration of play, then, takes place principally in elaborating the relations between means and ends that are under the child's own control and whose relations he can observe for himself. At the other extreme are those unstructured, informal activities that may indeed provide a group feeling but do not challenge the child's elaborative capacities. Between the two come activities whose significance we shall consider a bit later – pretend games, small-scale-toy play, sand and dough.

What social settings produce such play elaboration? The solo child in preschool surroundings rarely engages in activities that stretch his capacities. Groups of three or more children playing together do better at elaborating. But the *best* social setting for elaborated play is the *pair*. Where rich play is concerned, two is company. This is particularly striking for younger children, but it also holds for the older ones. Preschool children are at their most productive when they are in the company of one other child, even though the two of them may not necessarily be cooperating but only playing in parallel at similar tasks. Are larger groups too distracting, too complex for young children to manage? As for the solo child, he may be biding his time, he may be awed by the din of it all, he may be withdrawn. Whichever, he is less likely to be playing in an elaborated way.

And for the older children, playing with an adult is even more stimulating than being with another child. Would that there were more of it, as we shall see. It was surprising to find what a high proportion of adult-initiated interaction with children was given over to the boring stuff of petty management – housekeeping talk about milk time, instructions about picking up, washing, and the like. Perhaps it is a necessary component of management, but it is telling that the *majority* of contacts between adult and child are of this order. It is rare to find an adult inviting a child to richer play – in spite of the fact that when they do so they achieve such striking results, especially with the older group of children, as we shall see.

Talk and conversation

What about talk in the preschool? By now it is a truism that most parents hope that their children will have an opportunity to improve their linguistic skills at preschool. SRP explored, among other things, the amount of conversation and what prompted it. Conversation for SRP involved at least a 'three-element exchange on a single topic': A talks to B, B replies, and A then responds to B's response.

To begin with, of 9,600 half minute periods observed, only 20 per cent contain such conversations. This is not a high figure. Yet there is a fair amount of chatter in the ordinary nursery school or playgroup. This suggests that most of it consists of single remarks in passing or, at most, simple exchanges. One gets the impression that most preschools even militate against more prolonged exchanges by sheer social distraction. It is not that talk is absent – quite to the contrary. Rather it is that playgroups, nursery schools and nursery classes are organized in such a way that it is very difficult for *connected* conversation to occur. It is revealing that the places where longer dialogues occur most frequently are in what might be called dens, small quiet rooms or, indeed, enclosures that children make by draping curtains or blankets over chairs. Richer dialogue seems to require more intimate and continuous settings than most preschools now provide. When one examines videotapes of ordinary nursery schools and playgroups (as Barbara Tizard recently has in London) and compares the same children on videotape at home, there is little question that there is far more connected discourse in the latter. If connected discourse is the forge in which conversational skill is fashioned – and the evidence overwhelmingly points that way, then the interruptions and good-hearted din of the preschool is surely not ideal – however much it may prepare the child for the rough and tumble of getting a word in edgewise, or making oneself heard over the voices of others.

Teachers talking 'non-managerially' with children can and do produce long and rich dialogues. But management duties most often preclude such dialogue. And for chillingly good reason when one computes the statistics of the situation. Take the typical preschool group – any of the three kinds. It will contain, say, 25 children and three adult staff. SRP compute that on average, a child will talk conversationally three minutes in an hour with an adult. Assume that for each child each hour this constitutes three three-turn conversations with an adult. For the 25 children, this generates 75 adult-partnered conversations each hour. Assume these are equally divided among the three adults in the room. This makes about 25 connected conversations for each adult each hour! This leaves out of account all 'one-shots' or pair exchanges about milk-time and wash-up. Is it realistic to expect much more conversational activity from a teacher in preschool settings as now organized? And the records of the SPR study do *not* support the hope that the occasional visiting parent fills the conversational gap. If there is conversation with an adult it is far more likely to be the teacher and not the visitor who brings it off. They are the ones the children know and to whom they will turn. But lest the role of the adult in sustaining conversation get out of perspective, it is worth the reminder that two thirds of the children's more elaborated exchanges are not with adults at all but with other children.

SRP inquired into the kinds of activities in which conversational talk was most likely to occur. Recall, before considering this question, that 80 per cent of the nearly 10,000 half-minute bits that were recorded had no sustained conversation in them, so we are really asking about the setting in which a relatively rare event occurred. Interestingly enough, conversations occur in just those situations where there is relatively *little* intellectual challenge. When a child is thinking hard about what he's doing, elaborating his play, he is not *talking* about it but *doing* it. (The exception, of course, is pretend play.) So while structured tasks with real-world feedback lead to concentration of attention, relatively loosely knit, intellectually undemanding activities lead to good connected talk. Two thirds of the sustained conversations (again remembering that they are a relative rarity) occur in the horsing-around forms of gross motor play, in pretend activities, in situations involving working with clay or dough, and in 'chats' (defined by SRP as social exchanges for their own sake involving neither task nor other play). Pretend play, the exception, depends upon talk for its elaboration when it is carried out in pairs or larger groups, though one does not find that much of it. It has the distinguishing property of producing both richly elaborated play and rich, connected talk (cf. Garvey, 1977).

Talk is also far more likely to occur with an adult in those tasks involving the putting together of means to reach a goal. These are more likely to be initiated by the child. He is much readier to talk to an adult than a child while working, say, on an art production to tap the adult's resources or seek approval or legitimation.

'Chats' are a rather interesting form of talk – talk for its own sake. Sometimes they are occasions on which the child brings the out-of-school into the school setting – what he did or what his parents did or what happened away from school, two or more children comparing notes. But often children talk easily to each other and to adults about such tangible matters as a new pair of boots or mittens. But interestingly, chats need intimate or easy 'places' in which to occur – either the dens mentioned earlier or loosely organized activities that do not rule out conversation. But chatting too falls victim to distraction. One has the impression that, given more shielding from distraction, there would be far more of it. It seems just beneath the surface, awaiting an opportunity to come forth.

To sum SRP to here, children are intellectually challenged by materials that have clear goals, means for achieving them, and feedback so that they can monitor their own progress. About half to two thirds of the activity the children take part in at preschools leads them into such higher order elaboration of their play – more for the older than for the younger children. They are much more likely to reach these levels of challenge when they are playing with another child in a pair. Sustained conversation in the preschool is much rarer. Only 20 per cent of time intervals observed contained connected conversations. They occur in more loosely structured, less challenging activities. In the 20 per cent of situations where sustained talk occurred, two thirds of it was among children. A given child does not converse much with adults, although the adults may be at it all the time with different children. Adults are in a curious situation. The demand upon them in the ordinary preschool setting for conversation and for management is already so great as to be virtually unexpandable, given present ways of managing.

Activities on offer

What kinds of play activities are on offer? If we examine the
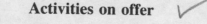

full 9,600 thirty-second observation 'molecules' that the study generated, and ask what activities filled them, a marvellous jumble emerges. We can partition it, for convenience, into eleven recognizable categories.

Activity	Time percentage (rounded to one decimal point)
Large scale motor and social play with low structure	15·0
Construction with building materials	9·7
Low structure manipulation: sand, dough, water	12·0
Art and music	9·0
School readiness tasks: books, number games, etc.	2·3
Pretend play with or without props	12·7
Social interaction without play ('chats', helping, etc.)	7·0
Adult directed group activity (e.g., 'circle time')	7·8
Watching and observing	9·4
Non-engaged waiting and wandering	7·5
Managerial routines: washing up, putting away, etc.	7·1

Table 5.1 *Categories of observed activity*

If we single-out those activities *most* likely to produce high elaboration and concentration in play (structured construction, art and music, and school readiness tasks), they come to about 20 per cent of time spent by children, about 12 minutes in every hour. It is not that other tasks do not produce *any* high level elaboration, only that these three we now know do so more than the others. The children also spend more continuous time at these tasks once started. We know this by examining 'bout length'. We can simply count up the number of continuous thirty-second periods over which an activity continues. The three forms of play activity already noted went on without interruption on average for three and a half to five and a half minutes at a time – these are long continuous bouts. They often were briefly interrupted, but they were then resumed. The figures give a good sense of children's commitment to structured tasks. Chats are typically over or interrupted in less than two minutes, gross motor activity in three, rough and tumble in a little over a minute, in contrast with self-selected art work (at about seven minutes) and building with structured materials (more than five minutes). Even school-like tasks, often dismissed as boring to young children, go for bouts of a little less than four minutes at a time. All these times may, perhaps, seem short, so it is worth a reminder that five minutes of uninterrupted play for a child between three and five is a very considerable bout indeed. Besides, these are averages based on many longer bouts as well as the very brief, glancing ones interrupted by boisterous activity round-about.

No surprise that elaborated play activity produces longer bouts of play than low level – on average four minutes versus a minute and a half. When children are challenged to higher activity, they stick with it longer.

The presence of an adult matters – even a passive adult not interacting with the child. The average bout length for children with no adult nearby is a bit over a minute-and-a-half. With an adult present but not interacting it lasts roughly twice that long. (It is irrelevant to compare the prolonging effect of an adult on a child's activity when she is interacting with a child, since the adult often has the objective of changing the child's behaviour to something else). In any case, whatever the dicta of different schools of nursery thought, adults do seem to operate as buffers against distraction, their mere presence serving to double bout lengths. And, of course, they also entice the children into more complex play.

Conversation among children helps prolong activity. When there is a three-exchange dialogue, play bout length goes for three minutes on average; without it, it drops to half that. And conversing in pairs seems to help improve not only the quality of play, but it also lengthens it.

What leads children to move towards more elaborated play and to stay there once it starts? Again, adults get high marks as an influence. The chances of a child moving towards more elaborate play and staying there are consistently higher when an adult is close by – whether passively *or* in interaction. It is not a great difference (about 55 per cent of instances, versus 45 per cent) but a good reliable one. And it may account for a finding we shall consider later: the larger the adult : child ratio in a group, the more elaborated is the play likely to be.

What does make a large difference in increasing the elaboration of play is pairing with another child. A child alone is simply not as likely to move toward more elaborated play than when he joins another in a playing pair. And the perpetual loner is even less likely to elaborate his play than the child who plays with others – even when each is playing alone.

Nursery schools, nursery classes, playgroups

Do they differ in significant ways? What we have reported thus far from the SRP study holds for all three forms of provision.

Take playgroups first. Whatever their philosophy, they have certain realities that constrain what they can do. In the main, they are small, they have limited access to the outdoors, they have relatively limited materials, they usually occupy somebody else's premises and must put things away at the end of the day (to make place for the karate class or the badminton club) which means that they must start picking up before the session is over. They have, in brief, many logistical problems. It is not surprising then that they usually are marked by more adult-led group activity than the others. It is a response to the constrained space, the lack of outdoor facilities, the need to keep some order. Which is not to say adult-led activity is bad, for in fact playgroups do *not* take second place to any other form of preschool either in richness of play or children's continuous time commitment to it. It is just that they are different and the difference reflects circumstance as much as conviction, ideology, or principles. For example, the only instances of 'formal games' (nursery-rhyme games and various folk games of the kind reported in *Lark Rise to Candleford*) were found in playgroups. Yet curiously enough, adult initiative did not diminish the incidence of child-only groups at play. Children played in pairs and larger groups among themselves as much in playgroups as in nursery schools or classes. It is a happy result, if not a planned one. It becomes clearer when we consider nursery schools next.

Nursery schools are usually large. In Oxfordshire the typical pattern is for them to occupy a separate building complete with kitchen and directed by a Nursery Head. They have good outdoor spaces and usually good indoor space as well, and the picking up routines are not so demanding. Access to materials and to outdoor space is conspicuously greater than in either of the other type of centre. Materials are in more profusion. Nursery schools tend to be run by a professional of considerably more authority than others on the staff and the head teacher is a real presence and authority figure compared to anybody on the playgroup scene. At this moment in history, at least in Oxfordshire, nursery schools place strong emphasis upon expression. This usually implies less constraint on the activities of the children. In any case, partly thanks to the space and partly to the ideal of expressiveness, nursery schools produce more gross motor play and more rough and tumble social play than any of the others. Such play, we now know, is less likely to lead to high concentration and to elaboration of play themes. Was it planned that way? And in the following section, we shall see that play of this type may require more managerial activity in the staff – with less time for non-managerial interaction with children. All of which is not to say that nursery schools do a poor job. Far from it. But do they do well enough, given their resources?

Nursery classes are smaller in size than nursery schools. They are formally under the authority of an infant or primary school, whose head is responsible for their conduct. Most feel more autonomous as a result, and may feel less the weight of supervision felt by teachers in a nursery school. They are peers with each other. But like playgroups, they are rather short on access to materials and to outdoor space. But they own their own space and do not have to get it ready to hand over at the end of each session. But their space is part of a school and there tends to be a more school-like atmosphere, and possibly more emphasis on verbal activity. Perhaps their solution to the relative lack of space and facilities and the school-like atmosphere is to specialize more in pretend play either of the dramatic type or with the props of miniature toys and dolls. Perhaps the gentler sociability of the school-room atmosphere favours the cultivation of pretend play by its very quiet. In any case, nursery classes lead the others in it. Perhaps this is what leads to the greater amount of child-to-child dialogue and pair formation in nursery classes. It is difficult to know.

I will be forgiven if I say, not without kindness, that I have never heard practitioners in the three settings talk realistically about what their setting forces them to do. Mostly, they do not know much about the other settings and perhaps it is true that the fish will be the last to discover water. In fact, all three types of school do quite well in a variety of activities, even given the unexpected specialization that shows up in the data of SRP. The specializations have costs: the highest proportion of solo children are found in nursery schools, and play elaboration in nursery school lags behind the others – the price for an emphasis on *laissez-faire* expressionism? The playgroups are challenging and elaborated in play, though they have been forced (by their settings?) into more story circles than, on cool reflection, they would be likely to plan for. On the other hand, such adult-led activity may lead to a passing on of more traditional games, rhymes, and so forth. It may also provide the children with a needed break from self-initiated and self-maintained activity. These may both be desirable, even if unplanned. The nursery classes reflect the calmer perhaps more constrained atmosphere of the primary school, but insofar as it encourages imaginative pretend play with its verbal elaboration, the result may be less distraction and more child dialogue.

Structure, intimacy, and staffing

Far more important than such labels as playgroup, nursery

school, or nursery class is the actual organization of a preschool – how it structures its activities, how many and what kind of staff it has, how many children, and less tangible things about its atmosphere. The SRP study set out to find a way of characterizing these matters and, beginning with activities, classified the nineteen preschools observed in terms of two characteristics that might be thought to affect the children. The first was how *tasks* were characteristically set for the children, and the second the *regularity* of the daily programme.

With respect to the first of these, 'task structure', obviously all preschools have some bit of required programme, if only milk time and a story or a required time for outdoor play. It is rare for such an activity to take more than ten to twenty minutes at a time, and they varied quite widely – story circles, number games, art work. Whatever they might be, they were in any case prescribed. The preschools, regardless of label, were classified into those that had two or more such prescribed activities of at least a moderately educational type in the course of a session, and those with one or less – call them 'high' and 'low' in task structure, bearing in mind, however, that even in the most highly structured settings the far greater part of the day was spent in freely chosen activity. Some very interesting differences emerge when the two are compared.

For one, it is *not* the case that the centres with high structure have more adult-led activity in total. If anything it goes slightly the other way. A second point is that where there is some required activity, there is a tendency for the children (particularly the older half of them) to play with structured tasks (construction, puzzles, small toy play, etc.) even outside the required times – twice as often for the younger children, nearly three times for the older. Required school-like tasks do not turn them away from such activity when they can choose on their own. Quite to the contrary. Interestingly, the children often prefer to continue on prescribed tasks even when the 'session' is over.

More striking still is the level of elaboration of play of

children in the two kinds of preschool settings. Even with the minimal criterion used for distinguishing high and low task structure, a steady difference shows up both among the younger and the older preschoolers. Children in the more structured settings generate more elaborated play than children in the less structured ones. And here again, SRP are referring not to the activity being prescribed, but to the free activity of the children playing on their own, as they did for most of the day.

It is not easy to assign a firm cause and effect. Perhaps it was that prescribed 'educational' activities set a tone, give a signal to the children, so to speak. This may be so. It may also be that the creation of a common focus for all the children and staff – if only for a half hour – provides a shared basis for conversation and interaction outside that half hour. Perhaps the effect is to lower uncertainty and therefore to establish somewhat more confidence in the children. The SRP figures do not resolve this issue – though they do rule out the possibility that the difference can be accounted for by the kind of children admitted to each kind of preschool or that, indeed, the prescribed, more education-al activities were actually teaching the children specific skills that they were then literally transferring to their free-time activity. In any case, the findings surely suggest an interest and readiness in the children for more intellectually deman-ding tasks. But the expectation of intellectually stimulating tasks also enters, as noted.

Regularity of routine was roughly defined as the amount of repetition of activity at relatively fixed times from day to day – whatever activity constituted the regularity. Regularity might conceivably have a steadying effect on children and thereby increase the richness of their play. It seems, how-ever, to have little or no effect on the children – possibly a slight aid for the younger ones in improving play, but of little magnitude. It is not of the same order as introducing some prescribed and mildly educational activity, however briefly.

Finally a more obvious matter: the question of staff-ing. Let it be noted that none of the 19 centres where observations were made was grossly understaffed. For the sake of analysis, they were nonetheless divided into two groups: those with child:staff ratios of eight, nine, or ten to one: and those with ratios of five, six or seven to one – in effect good ratios in comparison with excellent ones. If we compare the two with respect to kind of activity carried on, twice as high a proportion of time, roughly, is spent in the excellent centres in the kinds of activities that lead to play elaboration – play with structured material, art work, and small-scale construction: roughly a quarter for the upper echelon in staff ratio. And not surprisingly, these are the centres that lead in the quantity of elaborated play observed. Interestingly enough, the differently staffed preschools differ little in the amount of connected conversation among the children – in spite of the fact that the more loosely structured play in the less well staffed centres should have favoured it. Where they do differ, and not surprisingly, is in talk between children and staff, the better staffed managing nearly twice as much as the less well staffed.

And finally the issue of the size of a preschool. The 19 centres were divided into those with fewer than 26 children and those with more than that. Unfortunately for comparison, playgroups were over-represented in the former group, and in general the range examined was not very great. Even so, there were differences. The smaller centres seem to promote pretend play more than the larger; the larger more physical play involving running about than the small, probably because they usually have access to larger outdoor spaces. Where the big difference comes is in elaboration of play – 70 per cent of the play of older children in the smaller centres is elaborated, and only a half in the larger ones. Among the younger ones, the difference is less, but still present.

To review in homely terms, some prescribed educational activities during the day raise the level of play, so does a generous ratio of staff to children, and perhaps best of all is small size. Structure, intimacy, and staffing ratio seem, in the main, to matter more than whether the place is called a playgroup, a nursery class, or a nursery school.

How may we sum the matter up, before going on to the question of teachers and play-leaders? For one thing, lest any criticism be misunderstood, the SRP study leads one to the conclusion that the part-time preschools – whether playgroups, nursery schools, or nursery classes – are doing an adequate, if conventional job. It is hard to establish an absolute criterion by which to judge such things, but it would be fair to say that there is no cause for alarm. It is equally plain that there is plenty of room for reconsideration and thought where present practice is concerned, and we shall turn to this later.

The practice of preschool education is guided principally by conventional wisdom and there is little systematic use of research either to guide practice or to generate new ideas. Inspired social innovations, like the playgroup movement, appear to produce as good results for their children as are achieved in more established institutions, like nursery schools. Having said that much, one would then have to say that conventional wisdom, backed by concern for children may not be that bad a base to start from. There is probably more good judgement about children and their care distributed throughout the community than we have been prepared to admit in our age of specialization.

Indeed, some of the main findings of the study undertaken conform better to parental practices than to preschool doctrine. One of them is that to challenge children into more elaborated forms of play, you must give them tasks that have challenge and structure to them, that they can understand on their own, and that will carry them to the growing edge of their ability. If they are to be so engaged, moreover, keep down distraction and help the children buffer themselves against overload. 'Places' of their own where children can play (however improvised) provide one way to ensure such buffering. A single good companion as company is another. An environment where adults maintain a stabilizing, approving, and ready presence is a help. Large groups of children with few adults around can generate as much counter-productive as productive play. Some prescribed tasks that carry challenge provides a framework for a day that has a tonic rather than an oppressive effect on young children – whether in groups or at home.

Having said that preschools, as they now exist, give no cause for alarm (apart from the fact that there are nothing like enough of them), it is not amiss to say in what respect they give cause for dissatisfaction. Principally, it is the absence of a sense of lively purpose in what they are doing that leaves me, a somewhat 'outside' observer, rather bewildered. For example, we noted that many parents believe that preschool attendance will improve their children's language ability – and there are tests to show that preschoolers do better on language tests than matched children who have not been to a preschool (cf. Turner, 1977). In fact, again as noted, children's language in preschools of all kinds is most often far below their language at home, again citing Barbara Tizard's work (1979). There are, to be sure, programs like Joan Tough's (1977) and Marion Blank's (1974) on stimulating children's language, but the effects of such work on the ground in ordinary preschools and nurseries is minimal. And where it has been noted, it very frequently is transformed into aphorisms about what is good for children rather than into practice. In fact, the paucity of adult-child talk in nursery and playgroup *should* be a cause for some concern – though it is simply not noticed.

The elaboration of play, increased concentration, more connected or 'contingent' talk (to take our principal concerns in this chapter), are often taken as too gritty, too directive to be matters of direct concern in setting the objectives of playgroups and nursery schools and classes. And perhaps they are. Perhaps they should be the by-products of some other, more tender, objectives. Or perhaps they are, after all, rather old-fashioned and too work-oriented. It is also widely believed that, somehow, control of one's own concentration and full mastery of language will come automatically and in good season by dint of one's genetic inheritance. If that were so, the only justification for part-time preschools would be to provide some free time for mothers – which is surely an admirable objective. But there is evidence to the contrary that we will examine in the last chapter.

There appears to be much elbow room for the revision of preschool education in all three types of preschools. More high-level play and more protracted concentration could readily be ensured by the use of more structured materials through which the children can establish goals and monitor feedback. Such materials, if one's objective were to achieve greater intellectual skills in children, are plainly under-used. Data on concentration suggest that preschoolers are quite a bit more ready for such play than they are now afforded opportunity for. Similarly, if it were envisaged explicitly to increase opportunities for connected conversation, much more could be done to provide less distracting settings for conversation among children. And finally, since it appears to be the case that pairs of children playing together are much more likely to engage in higher level play, more opportunities for pairing could be provided. Preschool curricula are now usually a *potpourri* of activities, a rather all-purpose collection to satisfy all conceivable needs. For lack of a clear sense of procedure, this might be justifiable. But it is fair to say that it makes a rather flabbier curriculum than one might want for challenging children between the ages of three and five.

The use of teachers, group leaders, and helpers in preschools of all sorts seems to be poorly understood. As indicated, their potential impact on the richness of play, on the concentration, and the conversation of children is far, far greater than is achieved in current practice. The 'management' of children by teachers and playgroup leaders is a tender topic that deserves some tough-minded consideration – with all due respect to the deeply human concerns that characterize an adult's relation to a young child. In the following part of the chapter we shall turn back to this question.

One is brought to the irresistible conclusion that what is lacking is a network that makes possible the circulation of tested knowledge in the preschool world. What circulates now is a mix of conventional wisdom and scraps of research conclusions, usually untested in the nursery setting. Conventional wisdom is not lightly to be criticized. It reflects cultural values and often allows native wit to flourish. Besides, it appears to be producing tolerable results. Yet, one cannot resist the conclusion that far too little rational intelligence and informed research goes into early education. As stated in the opening chapter, there is no organized research community working jointly with the practitioners of preschool care and education. And short of such a collaboration, present research on young children is usually remote from the needs of practitioners.

A first ingredient for producing change toward a more rational planning of preschool education is surely the provision of means for observing children in preschool settings. How else can one judge whether what one is doing is indeed yielding the results one hoped for? The development of observation scales of the kind reported in this chapter and the preceding is a start. Such schedules can easily be put into a form that would permit teachers and supervisors to judge the outcome of their efforts. Our modest experience in Oxfordshire working jointly with teachers in preschools suggests that systematic observation of children creates a more reasoned, less conventional approach to preschool education. Indeed, as noted in the Appendix, the observation schedule used in the studies just reported is now being incorporated into the training of playgroup leaders by the PPA. It is obviously too early to tell how effective it will be. In any case, it is only a small step and it is patently an insufficient one. A more fundamental step would be to organize a long-term project that would provide a much richer opportunity for genuine collaboration between a network of preschools and an active group of research workers concerned with bettering the quality of care and education of under-fives in playgroups, nursery schools, and nursery classes in Britain.

Helping the nursery teacher

In the second part of the chapter we turn to the problem of how a teacher can change her own way of dealing with children to assure a better use of her resources for educational ends.

Recall the dilemma posed by the teacher's load. How many conversations can she keep going when she has 25 children to look after? We already know what a great difference it makes in the elaboration of children's play to have a teacher or leader available to respond to and support the child's activity.

The account on which we launch now is by way of a feasibility study to explore how a teacher or play leader goes about her educational goals, and how she can be helped to get closer to achieving them. I would like to report on a part of the study, conducted by David Wood, Linnet McMahon, and Yvonne Cranstoun (WMC).

It started with the teacher (or play leader) recording 15 or 20 minutes of her own interaction with children in the preschool setting – any 15 minutes she wished to record and after as many tries as she thought necessary to produce a fair or interesting record. The recording (done with a small concealed recorder carried by the teacher) was then transcribed and 'coded' by WMC. Bear in mind that fifteen minutes of such recordings contain a great deal of talk, interaction, and going about.

Once transcription and coding were completed, the teacher got together with a member of the research team – either McMahon or Cranstoun, both experienced playgroup leaders – and discussed the transcript, the coding, and in general what they believed to be the gaps between their intentions and what in fact happened. Many of them then went back and did subsequent recordings followed by the same analysis procedure.

Consider briefly some of the issues that emerged in this work – principally with respect to managing children in groups. Their own account will give a fuller picture of the work, and indeed it is continuing beyond the term of the Preschool Research Project.*

WMC take one aspect of the teacher's task as involving the 'management of materials, space, time, and interactions that enables them and their children to achieve substantive goals', and the goals they have in mind are concrete and finite: how to start and sustain productive conversation, how to get talk channelled into topics that are not tied to the here and now, how to encourage elaborated play, how to get children collaborating on a project, and so forth. Again in their words, the job is 'the good and careful husbandry of resources, of space, of time, of energy'. The goals, they note, do not come from the 'top of the mountain', but are the teacher's. The goals set will obviously take into account the interests and the capabilities of the children as well as the long-range objectives of the nursery school or the playgroup. But since long-range objectives can only be achieved by concrete short-range activities, they noted often that failure to keep an eye and ear on the goals of *activity in progress* (in contrast to a longer range objective or a management requirement) often led to confusions and poor husbandry.

Inevitably, there are two sides to managing and, roughly speaking, these may be called planning and response. The latter is more obvious and more easily detailed. It involves *directing* the flow of activity: providing services like aprontying, suggesting to children what they should do next, helping children out of situations where there is conflict about rights and turns, providing materials. In the WMC study, many of the recorded sessions contained up to 70 per cent of incidents in which the teacher or play leader was responding in this fashion. Planning activities are ones that project the teacher into other than a directive role: taking a substantive part in a conversation with a child, role playing in a game or in play, explaining how something works or can be put together, posing a puzzling issue or having one posed to you. Obviously, less mature children or less able ones

* See David Wood, Linnet McMahon and Yvonne Cranstoun, *Working with Under Fives*, Grant McIntyre, forthcoming.

demand more directive managing and there are also groups that generate more such demands. And it may well be the case – although WMC did not explicitly or systematically study the matter – that certain ways of organizing a nursery or playgroup produce more demand for management. More 'democratically' organized nurseries with more relaxed lines of authority dictating what *should* be done may, for example, generate more planful and less directive behaviour in teachers.

There are two causes of directive, managerial behaviour in teachers. One is more of the order of 'crisis management' – keeping property disputes under control, repairing bruised egos and skinned knees, negotiating terms, and so on. The other comes not out of crisis, but out of overly defined objectives – that 'this is "art time", but what Gillian is doing is not part of the planned art programme'. The latter type often, if Gillian cannot be ignored or responded to in terms of *her* perception of what she is doing, turns into the former.

There are three general findings about these matters that emerge from the use of the WMC technique with a few dozen teachers and playleaders. The first is that, in the main, teachers do not feel that directive activity is the best use of their time and, when faced with a transcript of their own behaviour, will often regret that they were led into so much of it by circumstances. They often comment that had they been a little more thoughtful, they could have avoided it. And often on a second recorded trail, they eagerly set out to do just that. And they often succeed, but that is a point that we will want to examine more closely. For their second finding is that teachers in fact develop reputations for the particular services they supply and children come to them for those services. Teachers with managerial styles attract children in search of management who do not come to converse or to play or to pose puzzles. In consequence, the children in a playgroup or nursery school may *prevent* the teacher from changing her role. WMC have several intriguing transcripts in which a teacher (on a second or later run-through of self-recording) is prevented from reducing her directive managing by children who have come to expect it of her.

The third finding, already noted in passing but worth emphasizing, is that in spite of the conservative tendency of children to lock a teacher into an expected style, teachers and play leaders *can* and *do* dramatically increase their planful activity and decrease their directiveness with the aid of the WMC procedure. As the authors put it, 'They are not "compelled" by their character, their situation, *or* their children to a high level of directive management; they can, with planning, set up their situation so that they can fulfil other roles if they so wish.' Change, when it occurs, most usually involves, as already noted, a better recognition by the teacher of what in fact she is doing. But let it be quickly said that this rarely takes the form of a blinding self-revelation about one's 'character' or 'type', but rather comes from a workmanlike assessment of what went on in the teaching situation that was recorded and analysed. It is not a new insight in the therapeutic sense. Change comes by the perspective one gains in observing one's own behaviour *after* the fact and *freed* of its pressures. The shift from *participant* to *spectator* may not invariably assure fresh perspective, but it surely helps.

How teachers get into their style of managing obviously varies. But WMC have come up with an interesting typology of these 'management styles' which, though caricatures, are useful in analysing this question. They speak of four 'idealized' systems of managing.

The 'pastoral' system

The adult takes on responsibility for a number of children who know they are 'hers'. Though the children may be free to choose and to follow through their own activities and need not be tied to their teacher, they can and do return to her in need. Meanwhile the teacher can keep some oversight on the day of each of her children. She also provides a natural link between parent and school, and mothers soon learn whom to come to to talk about their child. And the teacher may become a kind of 'school mother'. (Interestingly, many full-day nurseries explicitly use this approach to family grouping; see Chapter 7.)

The 'place/activity' system

The adult, rather than 'owning' a group of children, owns a room, a space, or an activity such as the art corner or collage table. Her territory and activities are known to members of the group, children and adults alike. Children who enter her space or come to participate in her activity are her responsibility. She may have little continuous contact with any given child, but they know where to find her and what it is that she has on offer.

The 'crisis-management' system

The adult is trouble shooter and she helps principally those children who seem to have got bogged down or who are in some need of assistance or direction. It is in its very nature a responsive system of managing and invests energy in remedies rather than projects. It may not fix a teacher's special role (e.g., as the arts teacher) but it can cut down on her possible initiatives where other activity is concerned. Withal, it is a tiring system.

'Mixed' systems

Most places and most teachers live in a mixed system (though one of the styles may be dominant). A teacher may be leading a story circle for a half hour, negotiating a crisis between two children at the water table five minutes later, and looking after *her* group of children at 'juice' right afterwards.

The major hypothesis that emerges from the WMC study

is that without the 'training' intervention they have employed or something comparable, much interaction between adults and children in groups is shaped by these management styles. A pastoral system, for example, often permits a teacher to see what is brewing with her children without her being involved directly and may thereby permit her easier planful intervention in their activity. But there are risks as well – as in too much dependence or rebellion being created. Crisis-management puts teachers into a directive role and the records show that they enter dialogues less often as a result. Indeed, the WMC records contain instances of peripatetic crisis-managers actually disrupting high-level play because children *expect* directives at their approach! Yet, as the authors rightly point out, crisis management is after all an extension of mothering and children may develop strong attachments to teachers who concern themselves with it. No particular system is bad or good *per se*, but too exclusive a practice of one system (and teachers often get into that inadvertently) may block a teacher from achieving other objectives that she also values.

And here is where observing one's own behaviour proves to be so useful. Take one interesting example – indeed, it is so typical that it could almost be a composite photograph of many such episodes. The teacher in question was very keen to get her children into elaborated conversations with her and eventually with each other. She herself wanted to give them some sense of the depth to which a topic could be developed. But over a period of weeks she had come to serve increasingly as adjudicator of little squabbles in her group. She noted with some frustration that she was conversing less with the children than she wished to. Going over the coded transcript of one of her sessions, she noted spontaneously that she was nearly always in the 'wrong position' for conversation – right in the middle of the most intense action. *That* was where negotiation was needed. Her solution was not particularly dramatic, but it was effective: in the next recording session she stayed away from the centre of activity when she wanted to start a conversation. Her presence at the centre marked her as a negotiator, led children to turn to her for that service and reduced her opportunity for conversation.

Perhaps the best way of illustrating the problems is by reference to the transcripts themselves. But though the transcripts are full of illustrative riches, one must take care in drawing any generalizations from them. They represent special circumstances. Recall that teachers could decide which sessions to record and to hand over. It is hard to know whether they did so because they thought a session was typical or because it puzzled them or because they thought it was a particularly good session. Yet, though the recordings may not be a representative sample of teaching episodes, they contain some instructive sequences of things that work and things that go far off base in terms of a teacher's intention.

Take the worthy objective of encouraging children into prolonged conversations with teacher about matters that are not simply here and now, but that are absent or in the past or merely possible. The first is a transcript in the enclosed space of a wendy house, a teacher and two children. It is full of elaboration.

C: Who's knocking at the door?
T: Hello. I'm your granny, I've come to visit you. (Aside – She's making dinner for me.)
C: I've made your dinner.
T: Oh you have, thank you very much.
C: (interrupting) I'm just sitting down.
T: I'm very hungry. Now, there's some lovely dinner here. You've been very busy.
C: Yes, I baked it all ——. I did manage. I've got *all* these babies.
T: You have got a lot of babies, are the others all asleep?
C: Yes. 'Cept these.
T: Expect they'd like some dinner too wouldn't they?
C: Yes.

T: Or have they had their dinner already?

C: No. That one hasn't, but those have, this one hasn't either.

T: Well, do we eat with our fingers, or with knives and forks?

C: Yes, oh no. (inaudible)

T: Oh, an egg, I'll take a sausage. I'll take a banana and a —— and a cup of tea.

C: Oooo! (inaudible)

T: (Aside – One of the other new children, Jamie, coming into wendy house)

C: I'm going to be the daddy now.

T: Oh, you're going to be the daddy, Jamie. Jamie, would you like to have some dinner with us? P'rhaps you could pour us some coffee. Try to find my cup.

C: We need some more things on the table.

T: Oh, perhaps we do need some more things on the table, yes.

The second example contrasts two conversations by the same teacher, the first done before the interview and full of crisis management, the other after, when the teacher purposely avoided immediate problems to be dealt with by handing them over to another teacher.

T: You finished, David? You have? Thank you. (Aside – They're all very quiet, I think they've exhausted themselves.) Karen, come and finish your milk, darling. Look, Mummy's just waiting for you there. Come and finish it. Hello, Sophie. Nicholas, your Ribena is here, if you want it. Well, Sophie, which one are you going to choose? Hm? Here's your Ribena, Nicholas. Now, which cup are you going to choose?

C: Blue?

T: The blue one, matches your lovely blue sweater, doesn't it? There we are, now we need some more milk in the jug, it's empty again. Used a lot this morning.

Debra, there's a chair there dear, look. (Inaudible contact – with other adult? – Thank you very much, you shouldn't have walked all the way back with them.)

It was very kind of you, thank you.

You finished, Lucy? Goodness, that's gone in a hurry!

C: I want some more to do a painting.

T: Yes, when you've finished your milk would you like to?

C: —— my writing.(?)

T: (interrupts) There's lots of time, there's lots . . . .

C: (interrupts) ——.

T: I know, I heard Mummy saying she would like you to bring a painting home. Don't worry, Sophie, there's plenty of time. Debra.

C: When am I going to do a painting?

T: Sorry?

C: I gotta do paint(?)

T: You don't *have* to just if you want to.

C: I got to

T: You would like to?

C: Yes.

C2: Mummy says, I *do* have —— it done up, at the back.

And here is the same teacher consciously playing quite a different role, consciously having changed her management procedure.

T: And were there many people at the fête on Saturday?

C: Lots and lots.

T: Were there?

C: Hm.

T: There will be lots of things happening next week . . .

C: (interrupts) And they had . . . hm . . . they had orchestra doing some mu-mu, doing some songs.

T: Did they? How lovely . . . .

C: (interrupting) And you see they had a singing (?) post and they had some wire on – on the bottom of the singing post . . . and . . . had it to the orchestra . . . Whenever the music stopped on . . . on the or— orchestra . . . hm . . . hm the . . . it was blank (?) you see . . . nothing . . . there was no music and then they could ta . . . talk with the microp . . . through the singing stick and then and then and it comes out big . . . in big writing (?) up . . . up in the orchestra.

T: Does it?

C: Hm. ———.

T: You mean it was a microphone?

C: Hm.

T: Was it?

C: Yes.

T: And . . .

C: (interrupting) They sing . . . with a micro . . . see they talk through the micro. . .phone (hurray!)

T: They did, yes . . .

C: And . . . all their talking went . . . through the wires and the orchestra . . . 'cause you see the wires was connected to the orchestra and you see (?) hm . . . the orchestra was, hm . . . doing some music . . . whenever it stopped you see, they could talk in the microphone all the way to the . . . orchestra (?)

T: It sounds as if lots of things happened.

C: Hm.

T: Was there anybody else there from playgroup?

C: Errrr . . . .

T: Or anybody else you know?

C: There was . . . Kirsty.

T: Oh yes.

C: And . . . Simon.

T: Simon?

C: Simon.

T: And which Simon would that be?

C: (inaudible – another child shouting.)

T: Simon Squires.

Yes I know ———.

So, it sounds as if you had a busy day – Hm?

C: There's three people going to playgroup(?) – me and Simon Squires and Kirsty.

T: Three of you from playgroup, yes. Mummy came too, I suppose.

C: Yes, and Daddy came see, to get ——— (?) but he didn't stay long.

T: Daddy didn't?

C: And he went to ballet.

T: And Rosemary what?

C: Rosemary and Daddy went in his car . . .

T: Yes

C: to . . . go to ballet . . . Rosemary to ballet and then she come back.

T: Yes.

C: To watch her, . . . to watch her and then . . . came back.

T: Yes. Well . . . so with four children in the family it does mean (child beginning to interrupt) you are extra busy, doesn't it?

C: (interrupting) Bu . . . b . . . hm, won some jelly.

T: Thomas *won* a jelly?

C: Hm . . . .

T: Did he.

C: And . . . and er . . . that stall where you have a pick and give them hm some people (?)

T: Yes.

C: Hm . . . hm some money. Then you have, hm, 10p.

T: Yes.

C2: Mrs Cranstoun?

T: (to C2) Just a moment.

C: . . . and you see, then, you see they have a thing with tickets in and you pick out a ticket.

C2: (trying to get in)

T: (to C2) Go and tell Mrs Harris.

C: Whatever . . . whatever number it is . . . and you

have to see what number, hm . . . it is on . . . hm . . . on the thing that you use . . . and I won, I won a sponge bag.

T: Did you? All the items on the stall had a little ticket on . . . .

C: Hm.

T: Is that right? . . .

C: (interrupts) And the . . . and the same ticket.

T: As you purchased . . .

C: Hm . . . hm in the tin.

T: Yes, I see.

C: One's the same. One ticket . . . .

T: (interrupts) But you paid . . . .

C: (parallel) . . . the same as another.

T: Have I got it right? You pay your tenpence and choose a ticket and then that same ticket is on some object on the stall . . . .

C: (interrupts) . . . and then, . . . and . . .

T: And you don't know what you're going to get.

C: And . . . and . . . whatever prize there's, that's the same as the ticket that you got out of the tin . . .

T: Yes you get!

C: . . .

T: Yes, I see.

C: You win it. And he won it on that and I won a sponge bag on that.

T: You were lucky, James.

C: And I've got some shampoo in it!

T: . . . something in it(?) when you bought it.

C: Four-year-old's (?) shampoo.

T: Oh, I see. (laughing)

C: Some shampoo for four-year-olds. Yellow —— it had a yellow 'four' on it.

T: Did it?

C: On one of the sides.

T: On the shampoo?

C: Hm.

WMC take a pragmatic view of what their 'training' does. It consists, after all, in reflecting on what turns up in a classroom or playgroup. That, they urge, is much easier for teachers and play leaders to do than they had expected. In time, they recognize not only what particular opportunities they have missed (or picked up) but which they *systematically* miss out on. It is then that they begin to see the roles they are playing or to recognize their own style. The authors comment that once this has happened, there seem to be three factors that teachers become aware of that help them find a role to play or a style to teach by.

The first of these factors is *group philosophy*: the ideals, goals and aspirations of the preschool in which a teacher works or with which she identifies. By its very nature, it imposes tasks and roles on teachers as well as aspirations. The more numerous and heterogeneous the goals, the larger the number of roles called for and the greater the likelihood of internal contradiction in what a teacher is called upon to do. More goals, they conclude, means more management and less disengaged time in which the teacher can enter into other roles of opportunity in play, in conversation, and so forth. Moreover, certain specializations in philosophy develop in response to the particular demands on a preschool. For example, schools with a longer day may develop more emphasis upon 'home-like' roles for the teacher, with more mothering, closer contact, and a background 'pastoral' system. Consciousness and clarity about such matters goes a long way toward encouraging workable strategies for coping with the teaching and caring tasks.

A second factor is the handling of the sheer *ecology* of classrooms and playspaces. It was a factor also referred to in the SRP study earlier in the chapter in connection with protected spaces being supportive of prolonged conversation, or cleaning up imposing constraints on spontaneity. If we take the ecology factor as including space, materials, interaction, and the organization of time, the four interact in a manner either to increase or decrease the need for directive management. Where few toys are available and space constricted, there is a need for turn taking and a risk of conflicts – which create the need for a crisis manager. There are many ways into and out of such dilemmas. And a problem-solving state of mind goes a long way towards staying out of them or, once in, towards helping extricate oneself. It is in this domain that the self-observation procedure was most helpful. And while many of the teachers who went through the experiment 'knew' about the sorts of remedies needed to improve their performance, it was interesting to them that it took the distancing of the self-observing procedure to bring them actively into consciousness.

A third factor in handling groups was *work sharing*. Some schools have well worked out arrangements for dividing tasks and roles among teachers. More often, there is a fair amount of confusion and relatively little discussion of the matter – particularly in playgroups. It can create managerial needs. Often, in the more hierarchical setting of an established nursery school, a plan for sharing can be undermined by the feeling of being supervised by the head teacher. Where work sharing is not taken sufficiently into account, there is the risk of everybody doing everything and nobody doing anything very well.

Can change be affected by consciousness of group philosophy, of the ecology of the playroom, and of work sharing? Wood, McMahon, and Cranstoun believe that it can. Their teachers *were* better able to carry out their non-managerial intentions and children did approach them more for non-managerial contacts. Their experience in the study led them to conclude that teachers' failures to achieve their objectives in conversation, instruction or play were virtually never due to a lack of *competence*. Perhaps their teachers were a confident and experienced lot. They did, after all, volunteer for the experiment. Even so, they could not be totally unrepresentative. They reported that afterwards they *did* listen more attentively to what children were talking about, they *did* intervene less often in an unnecessary way, and later recordings showed that they were achieving better what they had set out to achieve. They were better able as well to see the plights into which habitual procedures had landed them. The study has nothing to say about how long the effect 'lasts'. More to the point is the thought that some such procedure might be used not as a one-off affair, but that it might become a continuing part of the 'further training' of teachers.

Let me finally say a few words to put the two studies together – SRP and WMC, the one focusing from outside on the 'target child', the other from inside on the teacher's intentions and how she went about realizing them. Pressures of time prevented us from doing a study using both studies on a single group – examining child's play by SRP and teacher efforts by WMC. It should be done in the future: there are many questions that could be answered. For example, does a low frequency of dialogue among the children correlate with a high investment in directive management by teachers? Does the experience of the WMC procedure change behaviour in children as measured by the SRP observational method?

The SRP study found that the actions of teachers matter greatly in how well the children get on with their play. The WMC study found that teachers can change their ways in a manner that influenced children. Perhaps *all* teachers cannot change or cannot stay changed. Perhaps *some* children are impervious to how teachers conduct a playgroup or class. At least there is indication that one rational, not particularly radical, approach to improving playgroups and nursery schools is possible. Surely there are many other ways to go about it as well. But that is one of the main topics of the final chapter.

6

A view of childminding*

Childminders (to take matters forward from Chapter 2) are women in their own houses who look after other people's young children, who do so for at least two hours a day and for reward. By law, they must be registered with their local authority, though an unknown but possibly considerable number are not. There are few more controversial topics among experts on early child care than the quality of available childminding. It is poorly understood and richly politicized. That it is emotive stuff should be no surprise: not only are young children of minding age vulnerable, but their mothers are likely to be under the pressure of work and of personal problems. Besides, it is widely believed that childminding is a second-best resource favoured by governments more interested in economy than in fulfilling their obligations either to working mothers or to children in need of care away from home.

There are several reasons for our ignorance of what happens at the childminder's. For one, minders are not easy to get to as 'subjects of study'. They operate within their own homes and their privacy, rightly or wrongly, is inviolable. There are remarkably few studies of any kind based upon observation of behaviour at home, and the majority of these are on such neutral topics as language acquisition. Most studies of childminding have *not* been neutral. The early ones in the last decade were motivated by a concern that some childminding was so bad that it might do irreparable damage to children subjected to its regimen. Professional interest,

* This chapter is based upon Bridget Bryant, Miriam Harris, and Dee Newton, *Children and Minders*, Grant McIntyre (1980). I have tried to reflect the authors' account of that study but have doubtless expressed my own views as well. The reader is referred to their volume for a fuller view.

quite understandably (since much of it stems from social work) was directed to discovering and ferreting out bad practice, research designed more to alert the public to dangers at hand than to provide a balanced view about the nature of such care. Brian and Sonia Jackson were at the forefront of this battle to sound the alarm in the sixties and early seventies. In 1973, Mrs Jackson expressed the fear that 'backstreet' minders might be producing up to 6,000 eventual 'unemployables' per year in Britain. Brian Jackson reported in the pages of *New Society* that same year (29 November 1973) some of the unsavoury minding situations he had encountered in his research, particularly focused on unregistered minders. An example:

> In Birmingham, I met Mrs Griffiths. She kept six toddlers (four black and two white) on an old white linen sheet in her sort-of-front-hall for twelve hours a day. They did nothing; really nothing.

It was quite understandable why, in the mid-seventies, there should be such an expression of alarm in the social-work community. According to the DHSS, some 86,000 children were being looked after by minders in 1975 and to this day there is no clearcut estimate of how many unregistered minders operate. Much suspicion centred on the unregistered minder. For all that, what followed the alarm-sounding of the first period were studies on how to get minders to register and some work began on ways of improving the quality of minders' care. The heritage of that early period is the widespread public belief that unregistered minders are present in the tens of thousands ('between 100,000 and 500,000', according to a 1976 TUC report), and that their services are very dubious indeed. Indeed, a further and even uglier dimension had been added to the picture in 1975 in a report by the Community Relations Commission. The report, *Who Minds?* noted that white working mothers were much more likely to have their children in day nurseries and nursery schools than their black and Asian co-workers, who were forced to use childminders though often they knew the care to be unsatisfactory, sometimes indeed because the minder could not speak the child's native, only, language.

Perhaps it was inevitable that the pendulum should swing after 1975. For one thing, the early accounts were probably too unrelievedly gloomy. It also became plain as cuts were made in public expenditure, that minding was not going to be replaced by a system of day nurseries to care for the young of working mothers (or even, for that matter, of mothers in trouble). Childminding was gradually becoming *de facto* the principal provision for both. 'Realism' suggested that minding was something to live with rather than condemn, and the issue became one of improving the quality of the service. In any case, after 1975 the watchword for local authorities was the provision of 'support services' for minders, something beyond registration and inspection. These were envisaged principally in the form of courses and group discussions. Indeed, the BBC television series in 1977 (*Other People's Children*) was part of the same movement, though it had the additional motive of stimulating local authorities to provide more such support services for childminders. Interestingly, though most of the 'imagery' concerning support services took the form of providing education and information, no effort had been made to find what kind of help, if any, minders wanted.

Perhaps the greatest impetus to positive thinking about childminding came from the Sunningdale Conference in 1976, arranged and sponsored by DHSS. For reasons that were plainly more economic in origin than social or psychological, the emphasis had by then shifted to the 'realistic' theme of 'Low Cost Day Provision for the Under-Fives'. Now, even so distinguished a figure as Lady Plowden took up the theme of the minder as a proxy mother, and Brian Jackson, who had been among the first to sound the early alarm, commended the possibility of a system of minding based on good neighbourliness in which, principally, help would be provided by modest group discussion and short one-hour courses, supplemented by 'modest help' in the forms of toys, books, play equipment, and fire guards.

Yet, for all the new concern, negative and then positive, there has been little enough work on the nature of childminding itself, looked at as a form of child care. Such as there was gave little support to the 'back-street minder' as the principal source of trouble or to 'proxy mothering' fostered by the 'low cost realism' of the DHSS. Certainly the study by Berry Mayall and Pat Petrie that appeared in 1977 should have been little comfort to those who believed that registration and courses could turn minding into a first-class service. They studied only registered minders in four inner London boroughs, obviously favoured minders, 60 per cent of whom had 'taken part in some sort of training scheme', two thirds of whom were in contact with a social worker, and none of whom lived in what were considered bad housing conditions. Yet,

> The children led a low-level, understimulated day in unchanging, often cramped surroundings. Many did not get the love and attention they needed. Some had experienced frequent changes of minder. Most of the mothers were not satisfied with the standards of care offered.

And indeed, the TUC Working Party (1976) whose Report has already been mentioned in passing concluded at about that time that 'present childminding service is so seriously deficient that only root and branch reform can hope to achieve standards which are satisfactory'. They conclude that the cheapness of the service is illusory when matched against value received and condemn it as an outcome of the exploitation of minders who work for a pittance.

A few things emerge from research done thus far. Many parents put up with the services minders offer, for nothing else is available to them. Where the services have been looked at closely, they are often well intended but low grade or at very least unstimulating and, in more than a few cases, grossly unsatisfactory for the healthy growth of children.

This seems to be as true of children with registered childminders as with unregistered, and there is serious reason to
doubt that group discussions or modest courses have much
effect. It has also been evident since the short report of the
Cornwall Social Services Department in 1974 that childminders are no homogeneous group – that some are 'potentially
"professional"' in the words of that report, and some
transient, and that some are considerably more sensitive to
children and their needs than others. What Mayall and Petrie
show beyond any reasonable doubt is that, close up, the
minder is no proxy mother.

This was the background knowledge that existed when
Bryant, Harris, and Newton launched their study in Oxfordshire in 1977. Note it is Oxfordshire, an area with distinctly
less widespread employment of women than inner London,
strikingly less pressed for facilities, and probably more
prosperous economically than the settings where work on
minding had been done before. Balancing that good fortune
was a lack of support services for minders, even in the form
of 'modest courses'.

The Oxford study

The study undertaken by Bryant, Harris, and Newton (BHN
hereafter) as part of the larger Oxford project had a dual
aim – to discover how minding worked in Oxfordshire and to
make some sensible assessment of the quality of the care
provided for minded children. The study took the form of
interviews and observations of both minders and mothers, in
their own homes. The child was present in each case, and so
his interaction with each could be observed. The minders
were all registered and represented a random sample drawn
from the register. The interviews probed into such topics (for
the minder) as years of service, motives for minding, how the
system of registration had worked for her, how arrangements
were started and stopped; they also obtained data on social
class, age, education, training, previous work, and so forth.

Mothers were queried on many of the same social matters, as well as on reasons for wanting to work, work history, experience in seeking care for their children, and their assessment of minders and minding.

Describing the quality of care proved more difficult. It is a subtle mix of things: physical amenities, opportunities to form relationships with other children, the warmth of the 'atmosphere' created by the minder, the kind of talk that filled the day, the manner in which conflicts were handled, the relationship between minder and mother, and so on. Fortunately, the conversational nature of the interviews and the opportunity to observe separately both the mother and minder, each with the minded child, gave an opportunity to assess many of these matters, if some of them could only be observed glancingly. In any case, detailed notes were taken and there was ample opportunity to go over these at more leisure than the flight of interviewing provides.

In all, some 66 active minders were interviewed (sampled to represent each of the eight social services areas of the county). With few exceptions, they were willing to give us the name of the mother of a child in their care (who was randomly selected from among those they minded). Some 73 minders currently inactive were also interviewed, as well as another 26 who were no longer minders but whose names were still on the register. The purpose of this was to assess not only what drew people into minding but what caused them to quit. Just under half of the children whose situations were studied were 'singly minded' (that is, were the only child being minded – other than any children of the minder herself); the others were in multiple-minding situations, the usual number of minded children being two or three.

Interviewers also assessed the interaction of the 'target' child with mother and with minder. During a twenty-minute period, all approaches made by the child to minder (or mother) were recorded: touching, calling or crying out and looking, conversing, coming within a yard and looking, etc. At the end of the 20 minutes, the interviewer then filled out some 'summing up' ratings concerning the child's activity: his reaction to the interviewer's arrival, his principal activity during the period, how involved or detached he seemed, his mobility around the place, and his interaction with other children present. For the rest of the interview – beyond the twenty-minute period – interviewers recorded signs of affectionate contact between the child and his minder (or his mother): touching, kissing, caressing, picking up, and the like. At the end of it all, each interviewer took it upon herself to rate the warmth shown by the minder or mother toward the child on a scale from 1 to 5.

Observations obviously cannot be evaluated without a sense of how reliable they are – how much agreement there is between two independent observers. Accordingly, a certain number of interviews were carried out jointly by a pair of interviewers. More than 80 per cent of their joint ratings were within a single point of each other.

That, in bare bones, is the study undertaken in Oxfordshire. We turn now to what it yielded.

Minders and mothers: a quick census

Who are they? By far the greatest number in both groups were in their thirties, with minders being slightly older (33·7 years) than mothers (30·1 years). A good 95 per cent of minders were married, in sharp contrast to 78 per cent of mothers, the difference being, of course, in the nearly two in ten mothers who were divorced. All except one minder had children of their own, and they tended to have their first child earlier than our sample of mothers. And, as might already be expected from what has been said, the average family size of minders (2·6) was larger than that of mothers (1·7). Minders, being older and having started their families earlier, were more likely to have some children who had already gone off on their own, a rarity among mothers in our sample. The domesticity that characterizes minders is further emphasized by the fact that ten of them also had foster children in their care and a further eight had adopted a child.

There is a quality of rootedness among the minders not nearly so characteristic of the working mothers. Half the minders had lived within five miles of their present residence for ten years or more; nearly 85 per cent more than six years. It is enough to say that slightly more than half the mothers had lived as close as that to their present home for *less* than six years. And to make the matter even clearer, half the active minders had close relatives living nearby, the figure being only a quarter for the working mothers.

Along with domesticity and rootedness goes a social class pattern as well. Working mothers are better educated than their minders, and a few figures are sufficient to make the point. While only 9 per cent of active minders continued school after 16, 45 per cent of working mothers did. Or more concretely, in terms of 'marketability', some three in ten active minders had some qualifications, but six in ten of working mothers. Virtually all minders had been employed at some time, and virtually all had stopped full time work at the time of marriage or their first child. More than half of the mothers had continued full time employment *after* these milestones had been passed.

The best way of summing up the social class difference between minders is to note that three in ten of active minders were married to men in social classes I–III; six in ten of working mothers.

In a word, working mothers are somewhat younger than their minders, better educated, more geographically mobile and separated from their extended families, much better qualified, and much more involved in an outside world of employment beyond their husbands and children. They have smaller families, started them later, and went on working beyond marriage and motherhood. Minders are the other side of the coin: more domestic, more rooted in an extended family and more stable in residence, much more centred on home and family. In a certain sense, then, one is surely dealing (at least in Oxfordshire) with a group of minders who should provide a wholesome setting for the children in their care.

That picture is strongly reinforced by an account of professed motives for going into childminding. The great majority of minders started either because they were fond of children or wanted to have some others at home to play with their own. On the more adventitious side, a great many minders were 'triggered' into minding by being asked by somebody they knew or knew about who was looking for somebody to care for their child whilst they went off to work. They obviously were stay-at-homes: 80 per cent said 'no' when asked whether there was anything else they might have worked at. Very few mentioned money as a motive for minding – and small wonder, given the wages of minding.

How strikingly different the plight of the working mothers! The most frequently mentioned motive for working among the mothers who were sole breadwinners was financial. The study was carried out during a period of mounting, two-figure inflation and even better-off mothers with husbands working were feeling the pinch of mortgage payments and the like. Withal, there seemed to be another motive operating as well. A third of the mothers spoke of their boredom and loneliness, another group of the sense of 'being in a rut'. Nearly half of the working mothers interviewed voiced some version of the theme,

I got sick and tired of looking at four walls.

Not surprisingly, then, those mothers who said they worked because they needed the money, tended to work full-time; the others part-time. But it is worth more than passing note that only a quarter of our sample of working mothers spoke as if financial straits had *forced* them to work.

To return again to the general picture, the minder and the mother appear to complement each other not only in style of life but in motive, the one drawing her pleasure from life with children, the other finding it necessary as well to be part of a life outside the home. Indeed, we can say again that this complementary relationship might help the relationship of minder and mother to work.

A mother's day

Better to sense the context in which working mothers exist, and understand how they see the minding task, BHN interviewed 63 mothers about these matters, each for not less than an hour, and some for considerably longer.

The first thing to say about working mothers is that they are a hard working lot (including the four single-parent men) – and not simply because 60 per cent of them work full time. It is surely no surprise that holding down a job (even part time) combined with looking after a household and seeing to the needs of a young child packs a waking life full up and even invades the time for sleep. Still, the details of lives lived that way bring one up short by the tightness of the packing – and not just the detail, but the variety of styles for coping with it. Some cope with extraordinary zest. Take the thirty-three-year-old part-time computer programmer. Up at 7 a.m., dressed, breakfast with husband and two children of four and seven, dishes in the dishwasher and car loaded (this day including tennis gear) and off by 8.30, one child to school and the other to the minder – with whom she chatted a few minutes, husband then picked up at 9.15, and all at work by 9.30. Day's work done (including a quick game of tennis at lunch), at the minder's to collect her four-year-old at 3.45, cup of tea with her there, and home by 4.30 to start preparing supper to be eaten by the whole family at 5.15. After this, off with her seven-year-old to his swimming lesson, and not back until 7.30 when the children were readied for bed! Finally, 8.30 till bedtime at 11.00 she watched TV and chatted to her husband. She liked her job, liked her kids, had a good marriage. She managed to get her six-hour work day integrated into the rest of her life. She would have treated the suggestion that she stop working as absurd. Why should she stop?

But then there was the nineteen-year-old, not long married and with an eleven-month-old. Up at 6.15 to get ready for her full-time day working as a clerk (a job she found boring). While the others slept, she bathed, washed and dried her hair, got dressed, had a ham sandwich, and brought her husband a cup of tea in bed. While he was drinking it, she dusted and cleared up from the night before, leaving the house at 7.30, her husband to get the baby up and the minder to collect him. She arrived at work at 8.30, spent a boring day until 5.0, got back to the minder's at 6.0, stayed ten minutes and walked the baby home where she got him tea, bathed him and put him to bed. Then she began cooking for supper at 7.15. Supper was at 8.30, washing up began at 9.0, and after some washing and sewing she was in bed at 10. She seemed to get little more joy from her baby than she got from her job: he was 'grizzly' when she brought him home, she said, so she liked to get him fed and out of the way as soon as possible. Here was a grinding, leisureless and barren day with little buoyant about it. It was not clear what she got from working or whether, in fact, the baby was a wanted one.

But for all the striking differences in style and zest, one group stands out as having special problems: the 'lone parents'. There were ten single mothers, and three fathers. Virtually all were divorced or separated, though one was unmarried. They had no help looking after their children, or in taking them to or fetching them from the minders, no aid in shopping, or housework. And more than three quarters of them were in full-time employment. At the extreme, their lives seemed unbearably and unremittingly hardworking and driven – the divorced mother of four (aged nine, eight, seven, and three) working full time as a cook and managing the complex logistics involved without a car. In the main, moreover, they were (for obvious economic reasons) more poorly housed and provided for than their married sisters. Yet, having said all that, it must also be said that necessity also made them cope. Most of them *did* manage to sandwich in some leisure time, to see the occasional friend, to make labour-saving arrangements – the nine-year-old just mentioned did take the three-year-old to the minder's. Lest we leave the single fathers out of the picture, we should note that two of the three of them seemed to be coping with their problems rather poorly, unequipped as they were with conventional roles as caretakers, conventional expectations or for that matter with ordinary home-making skills.

Again no surprise: it was in the single parent families that one found the highest concentration of emotional upsets among the children. They, after all, were the ones who were living through the transitions that follow the shock of divorce and separation, and the transitions were often poignant with the usual human miseries so familiar in such circumstances. There seemed, moreover, to be so very little backup available to them for holding their families together – not even tax allowances for the cost of minders. Not surprising, then, that this group of families produced such a high proportion of the depressed and even withdrawn children whose problems we shall consider later. This is not to say that other mothers as well were *necessarily* any better off, even though they had husbands (and the nineteen-year-old married clerk with the boring job is a good instance).

About support and backup for working mothers, all 63 were asked about their contacts with social workers concerning minding or about their child. They were also asked when they had last seen their health visitor. More than eight in ten mothers had had no contact whatsoever with a social worker, either about minding arrangements or about problems their children were experiencing. And just half of the mothers reported that their child had never been visited by a health visitor. Given the pressures on working mothers, and given the worrisome behaviour of many of their children, this is surely a flimsy support system. Yet, harking back to our earlier description of services available in Oxfordshire, it is no more than a reflection of the pitiful thinness of such services as generally available.

Are working mothers taking these difficulties in their stride? The answer is ambiguous, and it would be as much an error here as elsewhere to simplify the subtleties that go into creating satisfaction with life. In fact, most mothers said they liked their jobs, though there were the expected reservations: 'It's not the job I'd choose if I were my own agent.' Yet four in ten had only good things to say about working, though they were given explicit opportunity to talk about the bad points as well. What they had to say about the enjoyment was neither complicated nor surprising, and three points cover nearly all that was said in reply to a question about what they liked about working: they enjoyed working *per se*, they enjoyed being in the company of other adults, and working kept them in touch with their profession or trade. Add to this the fact that one quarter of the mothers remarked explicitly that their jobs kept them from being lonely and depressed.

The picture that emerges from answers to a question about dissatisfactions arising from working is a little more puzzling. The most common complaint is the rush, the fatigue, the fitting of housework into evenings and weekends. This accounts for nearly seven complaints in ten. Surprisingly, only half mention the reduced opportunity to see their children. And only half that number (fewer than two in ten) mention possible ill effects on those children – such as making them more demanding or less secure. Could this be an accurate reflection of the state of mind of working mothers, or might not something be peculiar about what mothers are willing to talk about or indeed to think about?

For example, when mothers were asked directly whether or not they thought their children were happy at the minder's, *100 per cent responded in the affirmative*. BHN were sufficiently surprised by this unanimity to be led to read back through the transcripts of a sample of questionnaires 'to see if answers to this direct question of ours had given a true picture'. The question may have been too blunt. Few would willingly admit straight off that their child was not altogether happy in a situation in which they had placed him of their own free will! Interviews read as a whole did contain doubts and uncertainties. Sometimes there were strong statements of concern; more often there were tentative remarks about the child 'being a bit insecure, though she'll get better later'. Indeed, in some instances there is a certain pathos about it, as with the mother who, having hinted many times that things were by no means rosy, then answered the direct question about whether she thought her child happy at the minder's with, 'I think so. I think you can tell. A child can't be really miserable without [you] knowing about it.'

Interestingly enough, when mothers were asked what they thought their child had gained from being at the minder's, the majority answer was 'a chance to be with other children' – some six in ten. But the next most frequent answer, given by nearly three in ten, was that it taught the child to be away from parents – necessity, it seemed, had been made into a virtue. It is, by the way, rare for mothers to mention 'substitute mothering' among the gains: only about one in ten speak of the child gaining another loving relationship or a substitute mother.

Answers to questions about mothers' satisfaction with their present minders – whether she is doing a good job or not – have a curious ring. There is much satisfaction expressed: 70 per cent say they are very pleased, another 20 per cent say it's all right – though again there are many hints elsewhere in the interviews of dissatisfactions, usually not fully stated or developed. BHN comment on the curious power situation mothers are in *vis-à-vis* their minders.

> In essence they have relinquished their power and control to the minders for the time the child is there (with the exception of a few things they can specify . . .). The unspoken assumption is that the child fits into the minder's family's routine and rules and does not get special treatment. If a mother finds herself in disagreement and doesn't want to rock the boat, her best course of action, then, is probably to try to avoid knowing about what upsets her . . . . This is in contrast to the kind of arrangement whereby a mother employs someone to look after her child in her (the mother's) own home.

A similar pattern appeared in connection with a question on how mothers got on with their minders. The picture is strikingly less rosy than the one that emerged from the minder's answers (discussed below) to a comparable question about mothers. Nearly half said they saw their minders as friends. *No negative feelings at all were expressed in answer to this question, not a single one.* Nor did any appear in the rest of the questionnaires when they were reviewed. The authors say, 'We got the impression of some force making them not want to know about or think about them [the minders.]' The mothers were also asked – and it proved a most useful question – whether they saw the minder as somebody they could talk to about their own, the mother's, personal problems. Almost half did (45 per cent), but a revealing 55 per cent did not. Curiously, a far higher proportion of mothers than minders thought that they had the opportunity to discuss the child. Virtually all mothers thought they had sufficient opportunity. Yet, when one asked for detailed reports of the last such conversation the mother recalled having, they were vague. As for content, a good quarter of them either very infrequently or never talk about their children with the minder!

The picture that emerges of working mothers is of a hard pressed group, many of whom are coping quite nicely, a good fraction of whom are quite beleaguered – particularly those who are running households on their own or with unhelpful husbands. On the surface, they 'talk happy' enough about minders and minding arrangements. In certain respects they seem almost self-deceivingly incapable of voicing *any* criticism either of the minder or of the way in which their child is doing with her. Given what we shall see from the other side, it seems worrying to find among our sample of mothers not a *single negative remark* about the personal habits or standards or the personalities of the minders with whom they leave their children. It is hard to resist the conclusion that the mothers, eager to work, or forced to, avoid looking closely at the minding arrangement or the effects of it on their children unless things go badly wrong. What happens to the unhappy children in the sample, as we shall see, is that they become subdued, passive, too well behaved, and withdrawn. Unfortunately, it is a reaction that can be overlooked, but to that matter we shall return later.

A minder's life

What is a minder's day like? How does she see herself and her charges? What kind of environment does she create?

A first point, and we will return to it more than once, is that the childminder does *not* see her work as a job or as a profession in any strict sense. To her it is a sideline, work that complements and fits into her regular duties as mother and housewife to her own family. Minders say, and there is every reason to believe, that they enjoy doing it – and it brings in a little extra money besides. Perhaps it is this self-definition that keeps them from resenting the astonishing low 'wage' they receive – an average of 30p per hour per child.

They work hard and they work long – but it is neither something 'different' from what they would ordinarily be doing nor does it, in their eyes, require different skills. It is a continuation of domesticity. About two thirds mind 'full-time', a third 'part-time' with the figure of thirty hours a week providing the official divide. Again, some two thirds work five days a week, a few as many as seven, but 85 per cent work on a fixed schedule in the sense that they have the same children the same days and for roughly the same hours. The rest have 'supply' arrangements or other less regular schedules for minding. The minders' hours, while fixed in a weekly sense, are flexible in terms of daily schedules and they do not mind small variations in arrivals and departures. They are generally annoyed, however, when parents are very late or when they fail to notify them that children will not be coming. Perhaps it is a reflection of the low employment of women in Oxfordshire, but most of the minders did *not* feel overburdened by their load of children. If anything, the Oxfordshire picture was one of a shortage of children for available minders rather than a shortage of minders.

The physical setting at the minder's was anything but 'back street'. Virtually all were living in houses rather than flats, and virtually all had gardens in which the children could play. The houses were not luxurious, but they were well heated and decently habitable.

And socially as well, their situation gives every evidence of stability, a stability based on a primary commitment to their *own* family. Whether there were minded children or not, they were shopping, cooking, washing up, attending to children's needs, and it is interesting that nearly a third of the minders were occasionally looking after older brothers or sisters of their minded children after school.

Yet it could not be said that, for all the time and effort put in on family matters, that childminders are 'child-centred' in the atmosphere they create. The minder's home was adult territory in virtually all cases – living rooms with three-piece suites and expensive TV sets impose their own constraints. The kitchen provided, in some instances, a place for water play or painting. But the usual minder's household did not lend itself to the rather noisy and sometimes messy abandon of a playgroup or nursery school. The minder's, in a word, is somebody else's house where the child is staying when not at home. Indeed, so much was it 'another's family' that the minded children were, not uncommonly, taken for visits to grandmother, to friends, and these in turn would drop in at the minder's. It is most often a world of grown-ups and their things, inhabited by visiting children.

But the children were not at the minder's all the time. A good half of the minders took their charges to playgroups when their ages were appropriate and, indeed, it was not at all unusual for minders' husbands to lend a hand taking children to the park and for outings. And minders' own children seemed to enjoy the experience of other children, according to the testimony of minders who also felt that their own children benefitted from the experience of sharing with others. Half did mention, though, that occasionally there were problems.

BHN asked their minders to recount the preceding day.

Their account of common features reinforces the image of domesticity that is already so plain:

Although each minder was, of course, an individual, each with slightly different ideas, circumstances, and so on, we were impressed when reading all these accounts of 'yesterday' by features which they often had in common. The pattern seemed to be roughly as follows:

The minders would receive their minded children round about 8.15 a.m. or 8.30, and get their own family up, breakfasted and off to school by about 8.45 a.m., either accompanying them (in the case of young children) or just sending them off (if they were older). They would then wash up the breakfast things and tidy up the house a bit.

At some point there would be a trip to the local shops, usually combined with taking a child to school or playgroup. (Often the main shopping was done once a week or once a month, often with their husbands and without the minded children.) If there was a child of the relevant age, this child would be taken to a playgroup and fetched a couple of hours later. On these excursions out of the house they could have as many as three under-fives to keep their eye on at the same time!

Around noon, the minder would be preparing, serving and clearing away lunch. Often their husbands and older children came home to lunch . . . so this could be quite a busy time. They often reckoned to switch the TV on for the programmes for very young viewers, at about this point.

Throughout the day, they had to fit in children's rests, and special baby routines, where appropriate. Babies were generally fed at different times from the rest of the families. When the small children were having rests, minders tended to do jobs like ironing, which they often thought dangerous to do with small children around.

Then at about 3.30 p.m. there were usually older children to be collected from school, and tea to be got for them. They were then either in watching TV or out to play in the garden.

At odd times during the day, usually when there were only under-fives about, the minders would fit in their housework. They were often 'helped' by small hands when doing this and rarely had the chance to do it quickly by themselves. They also had to fit in preparing the vegetables for the evening meal (if the family all ate in the evening and lunch was only a snack) or giving the children tea and then preparing their husbands' teas.

Most minded children seemed to be collected round about 5.0 p.m. to 5.30 p.m.

This composite account leaves out the activities also included in the minding day of minorities of minders. One very important one is social visitors – we had the impression that a good many, although obviously not all, minders regularly went round to 'Nanny's' for a cup of tea, or over to friends' houses with the children.

The other minority group that impressed us was about one third of the minders who also took in young children in the 5 to 9 age range after school, as well as their minded children (under 5). These children often came at breakfast time, and were taken to school with the minder's own children, fetched at 3.30 p.m., given tea and kept for a couple of hours until collection by their (working) parents. Sometimes older children came in the school holidays, either full or part-time, sometimes the same lot of children, sometimes extra ones who came only in the holidays. So for this group of minders in particular there was always either a houseful of children and meals to be got, or groups of children to be taken or fetched from different places.

Surely one can only admire the organizational skills needed for such a schedule day after day. Small wonder minders mentioned patience and a fondness for children as desirable traits in their trade. They are probably the same traits a mother of young children would need. Not surprising then that minders defined their role as 'caring' for rather than 'educating' or 'stimulating' the children. This is typified in a predictable way when minders are asked what a minder should know about. Half mention looking out for accidents. A third state that it is enough to have the commonsense gained from bringing up your own children. The principal 'psychological' item in the list was 'knowing about children's play', mentioned by somewhat more than a quarter (a tribute, I suspect, to the playgroup movement). Children's problems and their feelings were far down the list. When asked what they personally would like to know *more* about, physical care and first aid were all that emerged; the majority of minders mentioned nothing.

Minders did not see themselves as involved in the problems of the parents whose children they minded. There was even a slight reluctance to discuss with parents how the children were making out: 'No, they wouldn't thank you if you did.' As BHN put it, 'On the whole it seemed that they (the minders) didn't see their role as having much to do with the parents, other than simply taking care of their offspring (often seen as a favour to parents, rather than as a job, as we have seen.)' And as we shall see shortly, this can and does create serious problems for some of the children in care. Take this instance from *Children and Minders* as symptomatic:

> After describing how insecure and unhappy the minded child was and how she wanted her mother all the time, this minder told the mother this and the mother said, 'Oh Flora, you're a naughty girl.'
>
> Then, 'I've been to her house for her to try to get to know me better, but she's still very inward there and wouldn't talk to me. She talked to me through her mother. I thought of stopping having her because she's not happy but then I thought her mother would only find somebody else and that would be worse for Flora.'

To put the matter in perspective for Oxfordshire, then, there can be little question that, by conventional standards, minders are well situated physically, they are the sort of motherly people who are able to extend the standard family routines to a larger circle of children than their own, they are domestic and well rooted in the local scene, and, on the surface at least, seem like the ideal counterpart for the working mother – who is less domestic, more ambitious occupationally, less well-rooted communally. Interviewers were impressed not only by the kindness and managerial skills of the childminders but also by the space provided, the gardens, the toys, the lack of herding – all rather in contrast to early 'trouble-shooting' studies and, indeed, even to the less rosy minding situations reported by Berry Mayall and Pat Petrie in London.

Yet, like the London investigators, and despite the superior facilities found in Oxfordshire, our study yields a gloomy picture of many of the children at the childminder's – again, often withdrawn and 'inward', unresponsive to the minder who may in turn then become rather withdrawn from the non-responding child, often passive and 'well-behaved' to a degree not corresponding to their behaviour at home at all. So we must turn now to the nature of the child's reaction to the minding situation – knowing that the issue is *not* a question of back-street minders with crowded quarters, not a question of unfeelingness or a lack of conventional motherliness, but something else.

What is the trouble?

The child's world at the minder's

Let me sketch the broad outlines of the findings first, and then return to the critical details. Roughly speaking, the sample of children studied can be divided into three groups. There is a first group of children who are noticeably withdrawn, subdued, and conspicuously passive at the minder's. When one observes them at home, the picture is not much better. They constitute about a third of all the children observed, and their behaviour is not an artefact of their having been seen on an 'off day', for in virtually every instance the minder's description of the child corresponds with the observer's. Well over half these subdued children are known to be having difficulties at home – recent divorce, family illness, some other upset. There is a second group of children – at the very least a third of those studied – who are also rather subdued and withdrawn and unresponsive at the minder's. Observed at home, however, they are ordinarily quite lively children who have a warmer relationship with their mother than they have with the minder. Again, their withdrawing response at the minder's is not an accident of time sampling, for they too are described by minders as subdued. Taking these two 'risk' groups together, we count some two thirds of the children in the care of minders in Oxfordshire. Troubles at home among children of this second group are not as ubiquitous as in the first group, but they are frequent enough to give one pause.

There is a third group, a 'happy third', who are not so much blessed with splendid minders (for it is difficult to find *any* difference among the minders of children in the three groups, and minders will often have one child who is coping well and another who is plainly not thriving) as with the security that makes it possible for them to be at their ease at home, at the minder's, or conceivably in any tolerable situation. Again, the interviewer observations conform to what minders say about these happy children.

This picture, gloomy though it may be, does not differ from what minders know to be the case among the children they care for. Minded children often pine, often withdraw, and often leave the minder unrequited in her effort to create a warm relationship. Minders are human; they respond as most ordinary people would to such a situation by 'letting it be', for in fact they must get on with their own domestic duties and with rearing their own children and the care of those in their charge as best they can.

Now the details. We had best begin with some general description of who the children are that we are discussing. The overwhelming majority are over a year old, and nearly three quarters over two. As one might have inferred from the earlier discussion of the stability of minding when we considered the minder's career, the children are not in 'fly by night' minding situations. Half of them are with the minder with whom they started, and where there had been another one, in a high proportion of instances, she too was a registered minder or, sometimes, a relative. Two fifths have been with their present minder for at least a year. Of course there are exceptions: a four-year-old who had started her life at the minder's at three months and was now at her fourth minder's. In the main, though, matters have been much more stable than that. We shall see, however, that given certain problems, the long stays may be concealing certain difficulties.

The children spend a lot of time at the minder's. More than half were there for a considerable part of their waking lives – and usually without benefit of school holidays. The average time for our sampled children was 30 hours a week at the minder's, and a third were there for 40 hours or more. Younger children under three were just as likely to be at the minder's for over 30 hours as were older ones, though the older ones (in seven in ten instances) had the relief of playgroups to which the minder's took them for a half day. Most of the children kept fairly regular hours at the minder's, but there were a few who had quite irregular, almost arbitrary schedules based on when mothers got nightshift work. Two thirds of the minded children had the opportunity of meeting and playing with other under-fives at the minder's, either other minded children or the minder's own, and our own observations as well as the minder's accounts indicate that close relations are often formed. But there are alarming exceptions: some 15 per cent of the children were not meeting any under-fives either at the minder's or in a playgroup outside. We shall return to this matter in a later discussion.

Do they have enough to do at the minder's? Certainly the supply of toys was adequate in quality and quantity, and even those few minders who were 'against toys' provided a generous supply of kitchen utensils. No discernible problem here. A third had rather low grade toys available (often at home as well as at the minder's) and a tenth of the children were really without any adequate toys at all. While there is little room to doubt that these children could be helped by more toys, the issue of toys is present but does not seem paramount. It could surely be helped, but seems not to be creating major problems.

So too for space to play in: in the main, as already noted, it is adequate. As the authors of the report sum up the matter,

> The majority of children were being cared for in pleasant surroundings, enjoyed a special freedom about the house and garden, and had reasonable or good toys to play with. Most of them also had opportunities to play with other young children, and to meet older children and a range of adults . . . . Most of them had not been farmed around from minder to minder, and a sizeable minority seemed to be in stable minding situations with minders who were not likely to give up minding suddenly.

At this superficial level there were, to be sure, some disquieting signs – like the substantial minority with no other children to play with – but thus far, save for the exceptional children noted, the external picture is notable principally for its ordinariness. It is a far cry from Mayall and Petrie's London minded children.

Now consider the more subtle but pervasive thing that we call quality of care. Recall the interviewers' ratings based on 20 minutes of observing the child while talking with mother or minder. Take first the matter of 'approaches', the child seeking contact with the adult. There are fewer approaches made to a minder than to the child's own mother, which in itself means little, since we may assume that the child at the minder's is occupied with other things – notably with other children. But it takes on significance when we examine the matter in more detail.

Take for example those children who, in the 20 minutes of

observation, made *no* approaches to the minder or at most only one. They make up nearly a third of the children. Who are they? Recall that a careful assessment was made of home difficulties minded children might be experiencing – recent divorce, death of a parent, a recent severe illness, real difficulty with the English language, reports of hypercritical or cold fathers. Of the 19 children in the study who had made only one or no approaches to the minder in the critical 20 minutes, 14 turn out to have severe family problems – close to three quarters of the group. This compares with little more than a third of the other children who approached the minders more frequently than once in the 20 minutes. What this suggests is that a major factor in producing withdrawal from the minder is unhappiness whose origin is outside the minding situation.

Could there be other, hidden factors contributing to this withdrawal pattern? Age? Younger children are as likely to approach the minder for contact as older ones. Children who have had other minders before (and who presumably might be worried about separation from this one)? They do not differ from those who have been all along with their present minder. Nor does it make any difference how many hours a week the child is being minded, or how long they have been with their present minder. So let us see whether we can get a better sense of how these withdrawal symptoms among the disturbed children get carried from home and get established in the minding situation.

A good three quarters of minders had kindly things to say about the child when asked for a characterization and many of them described the child's interests with considerable acuteness. Some of their remarks, indeed, were quite poignant, as witness the following:

> He's very friendly; not aggressive – he hates being hit; doesn't play well; very intelligent; lovely little boy but not quite right – he walks around sucking his thumb and doesn't like cuddles or kisses. He's a bit like a little adult.

She's a chatterbox: lively and bright and very loving – she likes an extra hug; demanding but quite adorable. I love her. She's a dear little soul. She eats very well and tells you she likes it.

She's very inward; she sulks; she doesn't adapt to other children – doesn't want to get to know them, not a friendly kid; not a happy child. Unsettled, just wants to follow me around. She's someone you don't want to get emotionally involved with; she needs too much security. (The minder felt this child should be at home with her mother.)

He's quiet. Intelligent but slow in actions. He enjoys playing with other children – gets quite excited (with them). He's a gentle little boy and gets easily pushed around. Got a nervous disposition – if I tell him off he wets himself. He doesn't do naughty things, not like mine.

Plainly, some minders were warmly involved with the children, though it is also true that more than a quarter of them had virtually nothing good to say about the child BHN had singled out to study, said disparaging things about him, and could give only the most meagre descriptions in answer to a question about what he was like. And indeed, more than half of the minders never caressed the child in their care during the observation period, or reported spending time actively involved with him the preceding day. Doubtless, the majority of minders had kindly feelings toward their minded children, though it is also clear that their way of combining life and work made it difficult to express those feelings in an active and selective way. And, of course, there was also a minority who felt no particular kindness toward their charges and had a rather remote connection with them. Add to this one other factor. Two thirds of minders said nothing in the course of the long interview that could be construed as 'sympathetic understanding' of the special problems of the particular child – which is striking in view of what we know about their home difficulties. They seem particularly uninterested in those problems of the child whose origins lie outside the minding situation.

Come back now to the three groups of children, the ones subdued both at home and at the minder's, those subdued at the minder's only, and the remainder equally lively in both places. If we now go back to what minders say about the children in answer to the question: 'What sort of a child is he? How would you describe him to a stranger?', we notice a very high proportion of answers containing synonyms for 'quiet' and 'detached'. As BHN say:

> The words they used varied, and we included any of the following: quiet, placid, contented, easy-going, good, solemn, moody, sulky, not friendly, dreamy, sad, adaptable, easy to please, passive, shy, reserved, no trouble, not naughty, inward, withdrawn. This list is, we feel, very revealing. Often these words were used in combination with each other, e.g., 'a very happy, placid child, easy to please, easy to amuse' or 'will adapt to anything really; never any problem; placid; always tired'. We did not count 'good' unless it occurred in conjunction with one of these other words as we felt it was not specific enough.

When we come to the three groups, we find four fifths of those children subdued both at home and at the minder's described in such terms, three quarters in the second group, and only a third of the ones lively at both places. So it seems quite evident that the passive and subdued behaviour observed was not unusual nor was it due simply to the presence of an interviewer on the scene. (It is interesting, by the way, that the study found no child who was livelier at the minder's than at home.)

Perhaps the best single indicator of the difference between the children in the three groups is the amount of physical contact between them and their minders. Only 13 per cent of the most withdrawn children had any such contact at all, in contrast to 50 per cent of those withdrawn only from their minders, and a full two thirds of the coping children. Recall that interviewers rated the 'warmth' of the relationship between the child, his mother and his minder – an impressionistic 1 to 5 rating based on the many clues a trained observer gets over an hour of interviewing and observing, yet withal a quite reliable rating. The three groups show a sad but telling consistency:

	Ratings of warmth	
	Mother rated:	Minder rated:
The 15 children who were very withdrawn	3·5	2·9
The 26 withdrawn at the minder's	4·1	3·5
The 17 who coped at both places	4·1	4·1

Table 6.1 *Warmth of child's relationship to mother or minder*

How to interpret this greater coolness of minders toward the withdrawn children? One obvious interpretation is that the children withdraw because their minders fail to show warmth – the more warmth, the less subdued the child. This seemed unlikely for several reasons. Some of the minders of withdrawn children were patently troubled by the child's lack of response and admitted having tried to 'reach him' but were unable to get closer. Many, indeed, had children in their care who were *not* withdrawn. Obviously, it is easier to show warmth to a child who approaches than one who hangs back, and that is what the withdrawn children were doing. It was principally difficulty at home that seemed to be depressing these children and causing withdrawal, and it was this withdrawal that created difficulty for the minder in reaching the child. Eventually, they stabilize in a kind of stand-off.

A number of minders (18 in all, about a third) expressed concern about the minded child – expressed specifically about such things as immobility and 'just sitting', about his prolonged silences, his tantrums, crying and screaming, or other signs of anxiety. Often their reports were clinically worrying, like the following:

> He needs an awful lot of reassurance; he's got it in his head his mother doesn't love him (she had left her husband and child), and I don't know what to say. He's

better than he used to be – he used to cry all day. He has a stutter and a lisp.

He's very withdrawn – you'll take that back to the office and say it's because he's being minded but it's not. He worries about his father hurting his mother or his baby sister – I don't know what to say to him. Also he rocks and head-bangs, but not so much here now. He needs a lot of reassurance – to be told I love him. He's fiercely independent and tries not to show his feelings – it's terrible to see in a child that age.

She used to be a bonny, bouncing baby but she's changed (since recent loss of father). Now she's very solemn, moody and confused. She can't understand – she expects him to fetch her. Now very anxious and worried, e.g., if her mother doesn't look back when leaving or is late collecting.

Very quiet and placid; better than she used to be. At first she wouldn't talk for weeks and weeks – just sat on the sofa and didn't answer.

Others were worried about language difficulties. For one in ten of the children had speech difficulties reported by both minder and parent and in some instances a social worker had advised speech therapy. Another one in ten were singled out by minders as causing concern because it was felt their language was immature. And these difficulties were concentrated in the disturbed children.

BHN estimate, using the most stringent clinical criteria, (only deeply disturbed language development or severe behaviour difficulties) that a quarter of the sample of children in the care of minders were actively distressed or disturbed as evidenced by crying, resistance, language disturbance, and depression. *All* the children with language difficulties and 10 of the 13 with severe behavioural problems came from families with known family difficulties. It seems fairly clear that the *origins* of the difficulty were not at the minder's, but at home. But having said that much, the authors then raise the disturbing question as to whether these difficulties are exacerbated at the minder's.

Withdrawal and detachment in young children produce strong reactions in adults. It is, alas, easy to take a 'snap out of it' attitude on the view that left alone in a kindly way the child will snap out of it on his own. And that posture is doubtless sensible under some conditions. But when it proved that this approach did not work, minders were not much inclined to inquire what lay at the base of the difficulties. Some of them saw withdrawn behaviour as unfriendly or sulky, passive behaviour in a boy as 'sissy', language problems as mumbling. And as already noted, it was not usual for minders to think in terms of psychological problems, particularly if their origin was at home rather than with them. This is *not* to say that there were not minders with both compassion and native therapeutic wit. It *is* to say, rather, that the severity of problems in the detached children often exceeded the skills of the minders in whose care they found themselves.

One other point. The study found that withdrawn or detached children were more likely to be the older (threes or fours) than the younger children – a tendency, but one worth remarking. It may be that, as many mothers believe, minding is an easier arrangement for younger children to adapt to than for older ones who may have greater need for the company of their peers.

It will have occurred to the reader that it is a bit strange that difficulties of such severity – affecting at least a half of the sample of children at registered childminders in Oxfordshire – should have been allowed to develop and then to persist for so long without some professional help being called in. There seem to be at least three contributing reasons. The most obvious is the lack of support services available to the mother. The number of social workers available for helping in such matters is negligible. Another factor is the absence of alternative facilities for mothers to turn to. And of those mothers who are living through difficulties like divorce, a death in the family, or other loss of support, the ones *most* in trouble, as any social worker and psychiatrist knows, are the ones least able to mobilize their own resources enough to find help – even when it is close by, as Shinman (1975) has shown in her study of how disturbed mothers fail to use available nursery and playgroup resources. Nor is it unlikely that some of the disturbed mothers in our sample were caught in just such a bind.

But there is one other factor that appeared to be operating that created difficulties beyond all of these. It is the curiously pervasive lack of any real communication between mothers and minders. A good part of the BHN study of Oxfordshire minders centred on this puzzling phenomenon. Let me sketch its outline briefly.

A good place to begin is in the initial 'choice' of a minder – with the word quite appropriately in inverted commas. In four cases out of ten, the mother (taken on average) chose her present minder as the only one she had heard about. In very few instances had there been any 'shopping around': parents settled on the first minder with a vacancy. In nearly three quarters of cases, no further inquiry was made once a minder had been found, and only one parent in the entire sample went so far as to take up references. What seemed to matter to parents was their own first impression – usually based on the minder's friendliness in general or towards children. All of this was rather surprising, given that there were vacancies among a fair number of registered minders in the county. Of course, it was true that a fair number of mothers were either directly or indirectly acquainted through a friend with the minder of their choice. Even so, there appears to be not so much a casualness as a passivity in choice of minder. Perhaps parents think that if the minder is a kindly 'homebody' that is what matters – and for the coping children, that is correct.

An effort was made to get mothers and minders to recall what was discussed at their first encounter. Responses were extraordinarily meagre. From minders: 'The usual things', or

'She told me everything I needed to know.' And from mothers little more: 'He was teething; when I thought he'd want to sleep and what he'd eat', from one who had placed her child only three weeks before. In addition, mothers gave telephone numbers where they could be reached and the name of their family doctor. There seemed, moreover, to be little thought given to settling the child in. In slightly more than half of the instances, the child started in full care within a week of the first contact between mother and minder. And 60 per cent of the children were left straightaway at the minder's without any transition during which mother stayed on. Indeed, most minders rather preferred the mother to plunge the child straight in: 'She should stay a few minutes just to get them settled in, but not stay a long time.' And there was little contact once the child was settled in. A few more than half of the mothers stopped to chat about their child when leaving or fetching him, but the others were as likely to rush in and out with the child or, if they paused, to talk about matters other than their children.

All of which is not to say that the children were not recognized as problems to be talked about. Indeed, of the 66 children on whom the detailed study was based, nearly half were *described* by minders and by mothers as having had difficulties during the preceding month. If we now take those children with 'recognized' difficulties (some 46 in number, including those mentioned by the mother, the minder, or both), it turns out that in only 21 of these instances had minder and mother discussed the problem, leaving over a half of troubled children neglected in any talk that occurred between minder and mother. And even where there *had* been discussion of difficulties, there were frequent reports from both sides that communication was not easy. Alas, it was about the *most* disturbed children (and mothers) that conversation was often the most difficult. Minders of disturbed children talking about their mothers used such expressions as 'unresponsive', 'very busy', 'very difficult to talk to', or 'she's not the sort to thank you for interfering'. Mothers were more specific in their complaints; they complained but felt they could not interfere. As an example a mother might feel the minder let her child sleep too much, so that he was wakeful at night; while the minder might say the child was so exhausted when he came she felt she must let him have a nap. Again, using a strict criterion, BHN conclude that 40 per cent of the children they studied had real problems that mothers and minders seemed unwilling or unable to discuss with each other. Recall that a broader sample of presently inactive and former minders were interviewed, and were asked about the conditions surrounding the departure of the last three children they had minded. This inquiry covered 122 children. Seventeen of these children were removed without the mother giving any reason at all. In one instance a mother telephoned a minder, who had been coming for her child for two years, to say simply that the child would not be coming again, either the next morning or thereafter. There were other instances in which termination seemed to us, though not so abrupt, to be based on failure of communication. Just as some 40 per cent of mothers and minders were unable to discuss the child's current problems, so it turned out that about 25 per cent of previous minding arrangements had actually broken down at least in part as a result of the same failure to communicate. Prior friendship between mother and minder was no guarantee of good communication; indeed, it may have added to the problem.

What produces this unhappy breakdown (or straightforward lack) of communication between mother and minder? Unfortunately, the study did not and could not delve very deeply into the question. It is a very charged one, and in the section following, more will be said about it in the perspective of what might be done. One good reason will surely have occurred to the reader before now. The psychological relationship between a mother who goes out to work and the woman with whom she leaves her child is never going to be an easy one for the two parties to sort out. Obviously there is some jealousy and resentment; it should be said right off that not much expresses itself in any direct way – though one may wish to interpret as indirect expression those complaints by each that the other was not paying promptly, coming on time, looking after the child's naps as she should, or whatever else was desired. We cannot know, and jealousy and personal resentment over a young child between two women is not a subject they are likely to discuss with an outsider, even if they are able to admit it to themselves. Yet, we should not be naive about this possibility.

More to the point is the culture of domestic privacy. Minders say that they do not wish to pry into the lives of mothers; mothers talk about not wanting to interfere in the personal routines and habits of their minders. Each sees her life as autonomous from the other – the child being the common ground between them. The minder, insofar as she considers her 'job' (and she usually does not see it even as a job) as an extension of her domestic routine, will naturally not see that routine as including being a social worker for the minded child's mother. And even if she wanted to be that, it is not her role. And so in some insidious way, the culture of privacy acts as 'the salt, estranging sea' separating mother and minder. And the child is often enough the sufferer.

That, in brief, is the picture that emerges: It would be less than candid to describe it as anything less than grim for a good number of children. It exists in a county fairly well off and where the minders are by no means a 'bad lot'. This is surely bad news for Oxfordshire, and one might alas expect worse elsewhere. Little question that Mayall and Petrie (1977) have described something considerably worse in the Inner London boroughs – more withdrawn children, more difficulty in communication, and physically and psychologically far less well situated childminders. How can we cope with such a problem as a matter of public policy – and cope we must?

Childminding and public policy

No use reviewing the tired topic of registration. It is the least that can be done. Nor is much gained by placing all hope in 'short courses' and 'discussion groups'. The London study surely suggests that quick instruction on the fly does not get much beneath the skin of minders. Our own efforts at collaborative research reported in the Appendix on page 200 reinforce that impression. It is difficult to disagree with the TUC Working Party's view that childminding wants to be looked at and reviewed 'root and branch'. But what can be done?

Should the mother of small children work? Moral indignation directed towards her will certainly not solve *her* problem. Nor will it solve a disturbed child's problem to put him back in the care of a mother who desperately wants or needs to take some part in the world outside of the home. The recent volume by George Brown and Tirril Harris (1978) on *Social Origins of Depression* raised the serious likelihood that increasing the feeling in young mothers of being trapped increases the likelihood of their suffering depression. So even if one were legally in a position to enforce the moral conviction that 'mothers of young children should stay at home and look after them', that measure might create difficulties of its own – unless one were willing to provide them support for their own problems. And certainly the lack of response to the Finer Report on the single-parent family gives no assurance that such help would be forthcoming. Britain's record is poor. Besides, there is some irony in the fact that, predictably, part of the prophylaxis that would be recommended against depression in young mothers would be to provide them means for being away from their children for part of the day. And if nothing better than present child-minding facilities were available, then we would be back precisely where the exercise had started!

Moreover, there is little point urging at this moment in Britain's history that high-cost, day-nursery care be provided for all. And, indeed, this means of care, which we examine in the next chapter, itself looks chancy unless carefully organized in a manner that requires a great deal of money, as we know. Public spending restrictions are such that it would be far wiser to concentrate on restructuring and improving the care that minders *can* provide – though it is undoubtedly (as the TUC Working Party quite rightly say) not as cheap a provision as one might hope for once it is reorganized to fill the requirement placed upon it. In the following chapter dealing with day nurseries, it will be proposed that until prosperity returns to Britain, time would be well spent in examining in pilot nurseries the shape that day nurseries might one day take. Such a delay is *not* possible in the reform of childminding services. There is no basis for believing that the trend toward female employment will be reversed, nor is there any reason to think that the desire of women to enter the broader society will lessen – no matter what happens to Britain's or the world's economy. Childminding is the principal form of looking after the children of working mothers. What can be done about it?

It is fool's play to make dire predictions about what will happen if the present practice of childminding continues. But the dangers should be made clear. There seems every reason for concluding on the basis of this study that the present practice of childminding will increase maladjustment in the generation exposed to it. We presently have no evidence that children at minders during the years before school turn out worse than others – none at all. Yet everything known about human development and about development in our nearest primate ancestors warns that early anxiety and insecurity about attachment to adults risks creating severe hazards in human growth. There are measures that can be taken to reduce these hazards. Indeed, even monkeys separated from their mothers and put on terry-cloth surrogates in isolation are spared some of the devastating effects that follow such treatment by being allowed to play with age-mates for as little as 20 minutes a day! There is quite straightforward knowledge that can be brought to bear on the improvement of childminding that has a good chance of producing results. Great cost is not involved. It would be callous at least and in the ordinary course of things morally corrupting not to make a major effort in this direction. The following proposals are offered as a way of opening discussion on the matter.

Minding and mothering

There is no reason to believe that minding somebody else's children on a regular basis is the same sort of activity as looking after one's own children in one's own home. Every bit of research that has been undertaken on this subject, including that reported in these pages, testifies to the contrary. Save possibly for a minority of children, minding does not work that way. An extension of domesticity to other people's children under your own roof does not necessarily provide the child with a psychological home. And if a child is having troubles at home, the minder is by no means a natural substitute for, or compensation for, what he feels he is missing at home. As the authors of the report put it. 'In all her experience of her own children, no matter how many she has had, a minder will never have actually seen any of them in the one situation common to all minded children, that of being *apart from their mother* and in someone else's care and someone else's home.' Health visitors, social workers, and education officers, (the 'old hands') are quite aware of the difficulties that can be produced by even a quite decent minding situation for an anxious child. The health officer of a major county in England (not Oxfordshire) reported to me that the withdrawal pattern in the minding situation had bothered her for some years, since she had found it producing mutism in West Indian children being minded, though mutism had been unknown in West Indian children – either in Britain or the Islands.

The minding team

There is currently no support structure built into minding arrangements. So long as this prevails, there can plainly be no progress towards putting experienced or professional care into the picture when and where it is needed, no means of ensuring some minimum standards in the arranging of communication between mother and minder, no way of alerting mother and minder to the need for special care. The answer, I believe, lies in the formation of 'minding teams'. The minding team requires at least the following components.

(a) At the level where the 'delivery of care' is effected, an alerted childminder looking after a group of children in a manner more child-sensitive than the present domestic round found in the usual minder's house. This depends on contact with the rest of the team.

(b) At a 'supervisory level', a properly experienced and trained 'visiting minder' (say for every ten to fifteen minders so that one day per week or per fortnight can be spent visiting each minder's) trained in the fashion of the *metapelet* of the Israeli *kibbutz* or in the fashion now proposed for *éducateurs* in the new French preschool system. His or her function would be to provide on-the-job contact and advice for minders. It would in my view be far more desirable to have visiting minders recruited from and indeed trained by a voluntary organization comparable to the Preschool Playgroups Association. The presently organizing National Childminders Association could provide the base for such a plan. What is crucial is that the visiting minder should not be seen as an outsider 'from Social Services', but that she should herself have been a childminder.

(c) The visiting minder should *not* have or be thought to have the function of teaching the minder how to mind. That would surely create tensions and run strongly counter to the ordinary minder's image of herself as a competent and domestic 'mother figure'. The model, rather, should be a more specialized one, relating to the interests of the minders as that interest has been expressed. They could be cast in the role of 'play tutors' (play broadly defined) as in such highly successful American ventures as Phyllis Levenstein's *Mother-Child Home Program* that have been operating with striking success for the past twelve years. There, the emphasis is upon showing the mothers play techniques, ways of interacting verbally with children, discussing developmental milestones, and so on. It is in this context that the child's difficulties and problems come to be discussed (although the Levenstein programme does not have a diagnostic and therapeutic referral service). Every effort would have to be made, as with the American visitors who consider themselves as play 'demonstrators', to keep a light touch in the relationship and to keep out of the picture any 'supervisory' function.

(d) The third level is a consultative and referral service to which, say, ten to fifteen visiting minders' would have access *as a team*. The service should include a psychologically competent health visitor, a paediatrically trained psychiatrist or a trained child psychologist, and an experienced social worker. This service, in effect, would provide continuing access not only to the dozen or so tutors, but through them to the 100 or 150 minders they visit and 300–500 children under their care. A *team* of a dozen 'visiting minders', in contact with each other and able to compare notes, would be far less daunted in their contacts with the professionalism of the diagnostic-therapeutic service than a single visiting minder operating on her own. Teams take courage in their numbers! Yet, the team would provide a ready channel for referral of difficulties to a central service locally situated — a resource not now available for minders (or for mothers).

The minders, visitors and diagnostic-remedial professionals would constitute a 'minding team' responsible for some 300–500 minded children. For every 100,000 children in care with minders, some 200 such teams would be required. Such networks would, I think, go a long way toward removing the reticence that now bedevils minding – both for minders and mothers – and could only be a help to children now having a rough ride. It might well give the minder a better sense of her job – indeed, might encourage her to see what she is doing *as* a job to be proud of.

There are many problems involved, but a solution such as

this one must come and can only take shape by trial and error.

Other children, other adults

It would seem on the basis of the observation provided by Bryant, Harris, and Newton, that attachment to other children is a highly important source of security to children at the minder's. Present arrangements, whereby children in their care when old enough are given an opportunity to go to nursery schools or playgroups should be encouraged and extended. Not only does it provide a child with other children as companions, but with other adults as models as well, ones who are operating in a non-domestic, child-orientated way, providing the child stimulation, challenge, and plain fun. Indeed, it would be highly desirable to explore with such organizations as PPA and Gingerbread (the organization of single-parent families) the possibility of setting up playgroups whose hours and character better fit the needs of minders who, in addition to all else that is put upon them, must look after their own domestic responsibilities.

Careers

There is at present no career structure in preschool education or preschool care. Where anything approaching such a structure has been introduced – as with training schemes introduced by the PPA and often implemented by Colleges of Further Education, it has had excellent effects in attracting the interested and the competent into training for playgroup leading or tutoring. The sort of 'minding team' concept just proposed might well have the effect of creating the occasion for establishing such a career structure. There is presently, for example, no postgraduate training available in Britain for anybody who wishes to pursue a career in preschool work. Such training possibilities would not be hard to bring into being through CFEs, polytechnics, and universities. Indeed, the Open University has already started courses that are relevant to such a plan.

'Curriculum'

In Chapter 5 we explored what engages the attention and interests of young children. In planning for adequate care for the preschool young – whether in nurseries, playgroups, day centres, or at the childminder's – the lessons that have come from that study should be taken into account. It does not help children to let them wander idly or unengaged. Like other human beings, they need a sense of accomplishment and activity to maintain morale. Preschoolers need a chance to engage in tasks that challenge their growing ingenuity with things, their skill with people, their powerful needs to explore the world of make-believe. The issues that concerned us in considering preschools are the same issues that must occupy the childminder – once the deeper problems of childhood alienation are brought under some better control. Again, it is to the minding team that one would look for help in this.

Minders and other provision

Given the choice of minder or day nursery or other group care, there seems little question on the basis of the study just reported and other studies already published (Mayall and Petrie, 1977; Jackson and Jackson, 1979) that minding is riskier. It is particularly so for the children who are having difficulty adjusting to stresses at home, and of these children slightly more so for the older ones. Minding is not a form of care that produces zestful reactions in the great majority of children. A minority seem to thrive. BHN conclude that 'three in five children seemed to be detached and quiet and not involved at their minders, and over one in four were

disturbed or distressed there or had impoverished speech
. . ..' They urge that their finding 'must seriously call in
question one of the main advantages claimed for minding
over other forms of day care, namely that it offers the child a
rich, loving, and satisfying bond with one person, similar to
the bond he has with his mother'.

We will return to this issue after considering the day
nursery, to which we turn next.

7

The day nursery

We come finally to the scarcest child care resource: the day nursery. There were too few such nurseries in Oxfordshire to permit a local study with any hope of representativeness. The day nursery, recall, is a staffed centre where a mother may leave her preschool child for the entire day under supervision as one of a group of children who are also in care for the day. In Britain such institutions are authorized and supervised by the county or borough Social Services Department. Many foreign countries have instituted day nurseries as the major means of caring for the young children of working mothers and they go by various names – 'day care center' in North America, *nido* or *asilo* in Italy depending upon the age of the preschool child, and so on. In Britain, it remains more an ideal than an available service.

While it is almost universally the case that day nurseries, in whatever country, are regulated by local health-and-social-service departments, they vary quite widely in their sponsorship, financing and organization. They range in pattern from voluntary associations created by parent groups, through facilities associated with colleges, universities, or companies, to official state day nurseries (as in most of Eastern and Central Europe) where training and procedure are laid down as part of a central nursery plan and where (as in Hungary, for example) there may even be centralized research in support of improving day nursery practice. Indeed, some Western European countries (notably France) have introduced special, nationally devised curricula for the training of helpers and supervisors in day nurseries.

It is generally the case that in the degree to which as a matter of national policy women are a natural and major part of the labour force, to that degree there will be state participation in day nurseries. State day nurseries, in consequence, are the rule in Russia and China and in most of the Socialist countries of Eastern Europe. In Hungary, for example, where 85 per cent of women between 18 and 55 are in either fulltime employment or fulltime studies, to take a case in point, there is no category of spare women to take on the minding of the children of working mothers. Unemployed women either have very young children or some other legitimate reason for being out of the labour force altogether. So jobs involving the care of the children of working mothers become jobs in their own right rather than leftovers.

It would take us too far afield to review practices in foreign day nurseries and the exercise would probably not be relevant. For in fact, it seems highly unlikely, given both the ideological temper and the economic scene, that this most expensive form of care (see Chapter 2) will gain much currency in Britain in the next two decades. It has become in Britain a form of care principally for the 'at risk' family rather than, as elsewhere, for the children of working mothers. Yet the British experience itself is interesting. For to the degree that *voluntarily* organized and self-financed day nurseries develop successfully (in much the same spirit as part-time care eventually developed) present British practice may provide a harbinger of things to come. And what will emerge is likely to be as British in its way as the voluntary playgroup is in the field of part-time care.

These were the considerations that led us to mount a study of some representative day nurseries in Greater London.* The study was designed, therefore, to get at both the *organizational* pattern of different day nurseries and the nature of the *care* provided for the children. There were bound to be links between the two. Two investigators conducted the study jointly. Stephanie White concentrated on organization; Caroline Garland on care. Both had stayed at home until their children started school. Both of them

* See C. Garland and S. White, *Children and Day Nurseries*, Grant McIntyre (1980).

were university-trained professionals in disciplines relevant
to the project – Stephanie White in the study of organizational behaviour, Caroline Garland in the observation of
behaviour of the young in groups.

Time and funds for carrying out the study were of course
limited. The decision taken was to concentrate on nine
nurseries in some depth. The nine were chosen after a
considerable amount of consultation in the interest of finding
representative variety. Three of the nine were ordinary state
nurseries run by London Boroughs, and these were selected
with the advice of local social service departments to whom
the object of the study was explained. They were not in fact
ordinary but were recommended by local authorities as
representing good practice. The other six were varied indeed. They comprised:

 a private nursery run by a charity
 an all-day playgroup
 a factory crèche run by a commercial company
 a nursery run by and located in a hospital
 a university nursery open to children of students and
   staff
 a 'community' nursery run by an agency interested in
   community relations

The nurseries were approached and the aims of the inquiry
made plain in advance of any first substantive meeting with
staff. The opportunity to decline the request for cooperation
was made easy. Few did decline. Stephanie White's interviews on the organization of the nurseries required an
average of three or four hours, usually divided into two or
three visits. It covered nine principal topics in a conversational way and with no effort to stick to a list of specific
questions. The topics were:

 the history of the nursery's foundation
 the nature of the service provided
 staffing and its problems
 details and difficulties of costing

the nature of the premises available

how the nursery was managed

contact with social services, educational authorities, and
    so on

relationships with parents

details of how the children were cared for

Needless to say, many topics other than those listed found
their way into the conversation. Withal, the interviews
provided a good 'management-eye' view of the nursery
enterprise, since it was conducted with the organizer of each
nursery and such senior staff as seemed appropriate. The
conversations were recorded in narrative form and provide
the basis of much that will be discussed in the following
pages.

Caroline Garland's approach to observation is perhaps
best put in her own words: 'The technique used, once the
observer had become familiar with the layout of each nursery, was to sit on a child-sized chair in a corner of the room,
and to record in a notebook what was seen and heard to
happen in as great detail as possible. Bouts of recording
lasted for 20 minutes, after which the observer stopped
recording for five minutes or so and merely watched instead,
to reestablish the context in which events were being seen.
The focus of each twenty-minute session was an individual –
more often than not a member of staff but occasionally also a
child, if what it was doing seemed interesting or relevant to
that day's activities in the nursery. Recordings attempted to
avoid guesses as to the internal state of the observed (e.g., A
was angry with B) but confined itself to description of the
actions and, where possible, speech (for instance, A bending
down towards B, shaking hand with extended forefinger near
his face as she speaks "You're a very messy boy . . .").
Shorthand symbols were used for many of the common
actions occurring frequently so that recording could keep
pace with activity.'

The amount of time spent observing in each nursery varied
from five to nine hours – the greater time being spent in

those nurseries that seemed to be successful in providing a good standard of care. There were two good human reasons for the bias toward successful nurseries that are worth recording here. Bad practices leading to distress in children are difficult to watch without breaking the rule that one must not intervene. ('On one occasion I broke the unwritten rules of observation by deliberately dropping my cup of coffee in order to bring to an end a scene between an untrained member of staff and a number of distressed children.') The second reason is that it is more difficult to describe and define what is happening when things are going well, yet that is where the challenge lies.

Because so many of the particulars of practice are part of the coherent style of each nursery, we need to begin by establishing an identity for each of the nine places studied. Garland and White (and for convenience I will once again follow the rule of using initials and call the study GW) give each of the nine nurseries 'titles of convenience', and their sketches disguise just enough to protect anonymity without violating individuality. Let me forthwith present their thumbnail sketches and pseudonyms, beginning with the three State nurseries.

> *Paul Street* was a busy, noisy nursery run in old-fashioned premises on the edge of a redevelopment site. Many of the staff were West Indian and so were most of the children. The atmosphere which was friendly and relaxed owed a lot to the Organizer who was outward-going and ready to take on anyone's problems. Her office was always full of people – parents, children, social workers and other members of staff looking for a word of advice. The children's rooms tended to be cluttered and rather shabby but relationships between the adults and children were relaxed and affectionate. Each afternoon a group of the older children were taken from this day nursery to their local State nursery school, where they joined in the afternoon session. There were 63 children at Paul Street.

Church Road nursery had a curiously enclosed feeling about it, due, at least in part, to the fact that it was housed in an old police station complete with cell block and asphalted yard. It was more than just a place of employment for some of the younger members of staff, who knew very few people in London and depended on the nursery to provide much of their social life in the evenings and at weekends. The Organizer wanted the nursery to be used as a focus for the local community and much of her time was spent in organizing social events, talking to parents and lecturing to students on the role of the day nursery. The children were organized into groups which each had their own suite of rooms and seemed to run independently of each other for most of the day. Altogether there were 37 children.

Vienna Close. This was by no means a typical State day nursery. It had been set up as testimony to an ideal and as a result was allowed certain privileges in terms of staffing and use of equipment. Its underlying principle was that it is futile to try to work with a disadvantaged child in isolation and they tried to involve the parents of the children in the work of the nursery. Half the staff were themselves unsupported parents with children at the nursery, and of the other half a high proportion had training in child psychology and psychotherapy. Their philosophy of child care was much more coherent and explicit than in most other places we visited. The buildings and grounds were attractive and the nursery was used as a show place for the borough. There were 46 children.

The remainder were private day nurseries.

Osborne Place occupied purpose-built premises in one corner of a large factory site. The layout and organization of the main room was reminiscent of a well-equipped nursery class and many of the activities the children engaged in were based on a similar programme. This programme was not devised by the nursery staff – who were all young and relatively inexperienced – but by the commercial company which the factory employed to run the nursery. The staff had very little autonomy. Many of the 40 children were from India and Pakistan and had not learned to speak English before coming to the nursery.

Nightingale House was also a work-based nursery but this one was run as an integral part of a suburban hospital. The staff wore nurses' uniforms and used their nursing titles. There was a wider age range of children here with more under-twos and fewer staff than in other nurseries of a comparable size. Physical needs were well attended to, but there seemed to be little time or inclination for cuddling and physical contact with the children, of whom there were 42.

Birkett Nursery was housed on the second floor of a large university administrative block. Most of the children's parents were students, so they were used to handling books and playing games like snakes-and-ladders or dominoes at home. They were generally a very self-reliant bunch of children – a characteristic which the staff recognized and were grateful for, because there were only two of them to look after 25 children. This nursery had separate morning and afternoon sessions and several of their children only attended part-time. The parents were responsible for working out a rota amongst themselves to look after the full-time children during the lunch period. Though there were 25 places, there were also some part-time children, so that in fact the nursery catered for 31.

Wilberforce Nursery was a specialist nursery which put particular emphasis on language training for minority children. Most of the staff were trained teachers; they were energetic and zealous in their efforts to stimulate the children both through activities in the centre and by an impressive programme of outside visits. However, the fact that preschool children need to be mothered as well as educated sometimes tended to get overlooked. The majority of children at this nursery came from ethnic minority groups whose first language was not English. It was a very well equipped nursery with a generous budget, and it catered for 23 full-time children plus two part-time.

Runnymede Playgroup was run in an ill-lit church hall on the edge of a redevelopment site, but the unprepossessing premises housed a particularly friendly, relaxed nursery. The Organizer was playgroup-trained and her helpers were all young mothers who knew each other and had children either at the playgroup itself or at the local primary school. The playgroup was only open during school hours. It was run on a shoe-string: parents helped by running fund-raising events; the staff improvised equipment for the playgroup; and they were all experts at bargain-hunting for everything from food for the children's lunch to paint and paper for art work. The emphasis on the formal aspects of education was less strong here than in some of the other nurseries, but the staff seemed to get a lot of fun and enjoyment out of the children. There were 24 full-time children plus six part-time children.

Marshall Day Nursery was funded by a foreign charity but was expected to be self-financing. It had attractive premises in a suburban house with a large garden and sympathetic senior staff, but lack of funds obliged them to employ volunteers as junior staff on a nominal salary. These young girls only stayed for a few months at a time and few of them had any experience of handling groups of small children. Consequently their behaviour towards the children tended to be rigid and authoritarian. The two senior staff were aware of the problem but seemed powerless to do much about it. Marshall had places for 25 children, but there were only 17 full-time children at the time of our visit.

The organization of day care

Before plunging into the institutional complexities of caring for children all day away from home, we would do well to consider the functions of a day nursery. Providing a safe and healthy physical environment is one. It is an obvious function, yet when is a child safe and when over-protected? And how much emphasis on health should there be?

A second object is a 'decent social environment', that in turn reflects on the implicit norms of the larger society. The thumbnail sketches of the nine nurseries should suggest that social environments created in day nurseries can cause as many problems as they solve. A day nursery needs to provide a good environment for educational growth. How down-to-earth is that? Educate for what? To teach the children of immigrants to speak English? To train for later school? Should a day nursery be educational at all?

Many of the children in day nurseries are at risk, with troubled family situations. They plainly need emotional support, a stable and kindly environment. Can a nursery provide such an environment without taking the family into account? Can it compensate for poor mothering by providing substitute mothering? The child must eventually go back to the mother, with all her problems. Indeed, the care by the day nursery may increase the mother's feelings of worthlessness and helplessness – both very much associated with depression in young mothers (Brown and Harris, 1978). These are obvious matters, all of them, and I risk boring the knowledgeable reader by mentioning them. I do so not so much to reiterate what is obvious, but to remind us of the complicated decision that must be made when one establishes a day nursery. There is in fact *nothing* obvious about it – whether one is talking about health or safety, about social stimulation, about education, or about emotional security. Yet one of the most striking things the reader will encounter in this chapter is how rare it is to find any explicit consideration of such matters in the nine day nurseries studied – and how good are the effects that may be achieved when they are.

For what comes out of the GW study again and again is that there are certain fundamental decisions that go into the organization of a nursery – fairly few in number, but highly pervasive in their effect – that express themselves from the start in the kind of nursery environment they produce and the functions they permit a nursery to fulfil. Indeed, it is not even plain that they are conscious decisions. We shall try in the following section to dissect some of these decisions. But what we should do first is to say very briefly how these administrative decisions (for that is what they are) work their way into the operating style of the day nursery. They seem to do so by affecting four crucial aspects of organization: what we shall (after GW) call *alliance, interpretation, control,* and *hierarchy.* A brief word about each.

The first, *alliance*, refers to a kind of contract between adults and children. It is an abstract word, alliance, but it is real in the world of nurseries. Does the adult see the child principally as an ally, as an entity to be managed or even as an opponent? In practice, it rarely is as polarized as that. Closer to life, it amounts to seeing oneself *enabling* the child to do his thing in certain ways in contrast to *keeping one's eye on him* for possible mischief. Obviously, the extremes are not as interesting as the subtle balances that form in this – as in the three following features. It is pervasive. It reflects organizational values in the nursery and deeply affects staff members. We shall see more of it later in the chapter.

A second feature is *interpretation* – how the behaviour of the children is seen and interpreted. The principal contrast is between the 'moralistic' and the 'psychological' approaches. Is the effort mainly to understand the intentions of the child or to judge his behaviour in terms of a moral code or code of rules? The admonishing, wagged finger that told the child he was a 'very messy boy' will not have been lost. Again it is the style of interpretation rather than the extreme forms that interest us.

Thirdly there is the approach to *control*. Is control of the child's behaviour done by direct confrontation and prohibition, with a *laissez-faire* attitude prevailing when neither of these is necessary? Or is control, rather, based on negotiable agreement about ways of doing things, with enforcement justified by references to a cooperative principle?

And finally, there is a distinction in nursery staffs: *hierarchy* and *hetairarchy*, working under a boss in contrast to a set of colleagues working together. It is a difference that signals itself to children in subtle ways in or out of day nursery.

Obviously, a positive alliance, a non-judgemental approach to a child's behaviour, a cooperative approach to control, and a collegial atmosphere in the staff make the stuff of nursery dreams and most nursery people will say it is what they are striving for in practice. And so doubtless they are, and there are times of success too. What we turn to now are the sorts of decisions made in organizing a nursery that seem to affect these four crucial elements in the style of a day nursery.

Well begun is half done

Prime among them is, simply, the objective in establishing a nursery in the first place. A good way to illustrate is by contrasting two of the nurseries that began with high and reasoned aims: Vienna Close and Wilberforce.

Vienna Close was founded by a group headed by a woman who took it as axiomatic that State nurseries were principally for the at-risk child rather than the children of ordinary working mothers. She argued (on evidence) that a day nursery could not be expected to compensate for the child's problems at home; that if those problems continued at home, the nursery could not equip him to deal with them on his own. It followed that the families, particularly the mothers, must be brought into the scene. This led to a simple plan of taking in six parents at a time for in-service training at the nursery. They became part of the caring community. A good deal of luck helped: Vienna Close was able, on the basis of this plan, to attract the cooperation of an excellent child therapy training centre, many of whose trainees worked there as part of their rotation. And many things followed from that.

Wilberforce had an equally interesting and ambitious founding objective. As a private nursery it had an option. Financed by an organization dedicated to the improvement of race relations, it decided to set up a nursery that would demonstrate how much can be achieved by creating a good ethnic mix at the nursery level in a community. Initially, it was to be community run. But it fell victim to an error in geography. The housing estate near which it was located turned out to have the wrong age composition, and provided virtually no children. It became known locally, for better or for worse, as the 'black nursery'. It had no community behind it and efforts to create one ran into the snag that a special support grant was given not to a community group, but to the community relations association who were financially accountable. A first director left; a second was appointed, and the objective changed to that of providing skills to disadvantaged minority children – also a good aim.

Wilberforce and Vienna Close were both quite clear about their objectives. And in terms of people taken on as staff, the curriculum, atmosphere, and indeed style of behaviour of the children in each place, each has gone by a path that was signposted by their original objectives. You take on more than you suppose when you decide to help distressed families or to cultivate survival skills in minority children.

Wilberforce has grown increasingly pedagogic and formal. It gives off signals constantly that things are businesslike and one must get on with it. The children are being taught and the teacher–pupil relation expresses itself in what we have called alliance and control. The staff is hetairarchic (and dedicated) and children are assessed kindly in terms of how they are developing skills (the general approach being Bereiter-Engelman). We will meet all of this in greater detail later.

Vienna Close leans more towards equal alliance with the children, its community is less given to a single objective and, on the surface, is less inclined to assess progress and

achievement than is Wilberforce. Again, the staff is democratic, but much more heterogeneous and less given to a
pedagogic ideal.

Each of these day nurseries, by any standard, would have
to be judged as serious and concerned – each along very
different lines. Each decided to be what it wanted to be.
Most of the others made no explicit decisions about what
they wished to do as nurseries, but either fell into a pattern
inadvertently, or as a by-product of some other decision.

Two of the private nurseries grew, straight and simple, out
of the conviction that women should have the right to work if
they wish to. Their aim was to provide care for their young in
a conventional way and without much soul-searching about
it. These were Birkett and Runnymede, and they are very
different places. One was set up by students and younger
staff at a London college, the other by young mothers in an
area of rundown housing, originally as an ordinary part-day
playgroup which was then expanded to provide full-day care.
Both were conspicuous instances of self help. One limited
the self-help concept to the founding of the day centre. The
other incorporated it into a means for providing care. The
former hired help and the latter provided most of it themselves on a rota basis. Both regard children as young allies; in
neither is there confrontation. Neither is hierarchical. Both
have worked well, the former in a constant if good-natured
state of staff shortage, the latter with sufficient staff, considerable clutter, and much good nature as well. They both
live within the constraint of their founding objectives.

Objectives matter. And so does the subtle process of
accountability – to whom is one responsible for decisions
about who attends or what goes on in the nursery, etc.? The
GW sample included some interesting contrasts. At one
extreme was Osborne, a factory crèche run by a commercial
company whose product was nursery care, hiring semi-
trained women to follow a rather traditional nursery format,
and a supervisor to assure that they did so. The objective was
to provide a 'package' of care for a fee. The contract was
between a care-providing company and a food-processing

one. Insofar as local staff felt they were middlemen between the company's curriculum and the children (with parents excluded), the situation was strikingly hierarchical; there was no positive alliance between children and staff, and control was intended to prevent trouble. The teachers were accountable to the supervisor who also defined what was a decent job of work. The young immigrant mothers working at the factory took what they could get.

Nightingale provides another instance of rigid accountability. It was in a building separate from the hospital proper, but its routine was under the supervision of the nursing staff, who were responsible to a Principal Nursing Officer. While it is not an inevitable consequence of the medical setting that order, cleanliness, and routine be honoured norms, in this instance the classic medical model was highly in evidence. Children's individual habits were regarded as disruptions of routine; parents were seen rather as one would see patients with idiosyncratic demands, with issues of physical well-being sometimes insensitively handled – as when, for example, a crying child was given a full feed half an hour before the mother was due to turn up for a breast-feeding, so that she then experienced it as a feeding failure.

And even at the State nurseries, where accountability included a share for the parents, at Paul Street and Vienna Close, parents at the regular evening meetings seemed ill at ease. And the staff there felt that they, the parents, did not have much of a feel for the practical problems of running a nursery. For again, the structure in both places, however admirable they might be, was based on professionals in charge and others helping out (or being helped out). This was in contrast to Runnymede with a playgroup-participatory background, where parents were lively participants in establishing policy and where executive power resided in a sub-committee of parents who could be and were called to account at meetings on matters of policy. At the other private nurseries, management committees were used, but these often ran into dilemmas produced by having to report in two directions – to the charity or organization that sponsored the nursery, and to the parents whose children were looked after. The effect was more often than not a rather feeble participating spirit on the part of the parents. And accountability in those groups turned out to be hard to define.

The two matters – initial objectives and accountability – provide, so to speak, direction and correction to a nursery. And in this brief section, before turning to the richer detail of day-to-day behaviour of children and staff in nurseries, I have wanted to make plain how important the two processes are in fixing the styles of these nine nursery schools. What happens later in a nursery is *very* much affected by the original plan, and how much one can correct for initial error is constrained by the kind of system of accountability one builds in.

If decisions at the outset were taken quite consciously, it would not be so very difficult to follow the advice 'Beware'. But interviews indicate that, in the main, the crucial decisions are not so much *taken* as fallen into without much explicit thought as to eventual consequences. They often take the form of little steps. But in aggregate they constitute a *foundation policy* of the nursery, and though this may sound a grand name for small things, its effect on the life of the children and staff is crucial. Policy is not much discussed when one is concerned with nurseries. Indeed, the sympathetic informality that the care of young children should evoke may inhibit it – and thereby make room for unspoken biases to find their unintended way into the running of the nursery. Certainly the main conclusion of the GW study, where administration is concerned, is that a clear sense of what one wants to accomplish and of the form of accountability makes a great deal of difference in whether the nursery gives children and staff alike a happy time of it. There are many ways of running a nursery that seem to produce a happy climate. But there are also many ways of making life difficult. We can return to these matters later. But lest we become too management orientated, consider the children in the nurseries.

A long day away from home

However different they might be, all the nurseries in the GW study had some things in common – perhaps the basic necessities for looking after a group of children the whole day long. They all had some fixed routines that occurred at certain times during the day, such as circle time or story time. They break the day into more manageable chunks for both staff and children. How *much* routine varied from place to place depending upon how much they wanted their nursery to be like 'the unpredictable flow of life at home'. Typically, day nurseries open between 7.00 and 8.30 a.m., although some children do not get there until 10.00. The first couple of hours of the day before milk time consisted of 'free play', a term susceptible, as we shall see, to widely differing interpretation. Usually this included opportunity to play with some of the familiar equipment available at all the nurseries: sand, clay, water, paint, and a Wendy corner indoors; or bikes, scooters, and balls outdoors.

Mid-morning milk was usually accompanied by a story, singing, nursery rhymes, or discussion of a topic of special interest. Two of the schools permitted children to watch *Playschool* after milk, but in general television was little used, and then principally for children's programmes after four.

After milk and until lunch, things become more organized – the water table might be used for talk about sinking or floating, or lesson periods occur, immigrant children might be given lessons in English. Lunch, curiously, was in all but one place left to the supervision of untrained staff, many of whom were part-timers, and consequently little was made of it. Obviously, regular staff needed a lunch break. Yet, an opportunity was lost, as the exception showed. The exception was Vienna Close. They made lunch a special event of the day, replete with male chef and a splendid meal. Where the nurseries were organized in family groups, these groups ate together. After lunch was a rest time, in most places obligatory, with children lying on their rugs or beds, though in some places rest meant simply being quiet and low key.

Then came an excursion or outdoor play, with the boys gravitating to the large equipment, the climbing frames and the bikes. The excursions varied from visits to the park or the supermarket, even to a playgroup or seasonally to a swimming pool. Wilberforce, keen always on the instructional side of things, went in for the most ambitious excursions. Nightingale and Osborne were constrained by insurance cover and could not take their children beyond the premises or the lawn outside. Others were lucky – Birkett that could use a locked garden in the middle of a London square. The afternoon was also a time for visitors.

Parents started arriving after 3.00 to take children home, but some children stayed until 6.00 – for a very long day indeed. Things slowed down out of sheer fatigue – of children and staff alike. A nursery day extends for longer than any they will have when they start school at five. It takes some doing to fill long days with variety, challenge and familiarity for the children – and conviviality for the staff!

GW report an interesting variety of styles in the way the daily slots in the routine are filled in. 'Free play' is a particularly interesting case in point. In general, the more structured the approach of the particular nursery, the more sharply drawn was the distinction between free play and particular activities. In general, the greater the emphasis on lessons in the set activities, the less the supervision of play. Wilberforce (with its emphasis on teaching skills to the underprivileged) gave short shrift to free play: it ended when all the children were assembled at the start of the day. Two others, big on lessons, had a ratio of one teacher to 25 children during free play. Runnymede, with its background as a playgroup, on the other hand, drew a much less clearcut distinction between the two – and had as many supervisors about for free play as for formal activities. Adult participation was not confined to more pedagogical activities.

What was particularly striking was the manner in which some nurseries imposed a label of 'work' or of 'play' on what children were doing. Which activity was treated as which could be quite different depending upon where you happened to be: in one place, adults labelled painting as work, or a lesson; in others it was free play. What varied was adult attitude rather than the activity. In one case the adults were usually 'telling how', whereas in the other the children were experimenting with the medium, with or without adult encouragement. But about one thing there was no confusion: in all nurseries, being occupied was felt to be better than being idle. That is a universal of nursery ideology and characterized all nine nurseries. At Runnymede one heard the refrain, 'Come and be busy', or 'Shall we go and be busy?' At Nightingale and Wilberforce, 'Make something with the bricks,' or 'Come on, build something.' At Church Road, 'Sit down and make something – you never do anything, do you?'

Once a child *is* busy, there is a certain predictability as to *which* activities produce response from adults. Painting, collage, puzzles, and other activities done at a table or at a set place were far more likely to attract the attention of an adult than unassembled activities. And girls were more likely to engage in the assembled ones – whether simply to be in contact with adults or not is hard to say. Since the GW study did not employ the time recording methods of the SPR observational study of playgroups and nursery schools reported in Chapter 5, it is hard to say precisely how adult attention was distributed over activities. All we can say is that adults tended to hover around set activities and ignore spontaneously generated play. And how quickly the former were infiltrated with adult teaching techniques in which there was a 'right way' of doing the job! The GW observational records are full of examples. At Wilberforce a pastry making session around a table was instructed with respect to the shape of the pastries, their colour, the degree of messiness encountered, and the degree of terminal stickiness. Adult-child conversation, accordingly, was adult dominated and principally instructional in tone. And at Osborne, children queued for their turn at the finger paint table, and were instructed on how to spread the paint; before the teacher made a paper print, and sent the child off to wash his hands – all in three minutes per child. Yet at some of the nurseries there was a distinct spirit of letting the child keep the initiative, providing technique to help the child to his own artistic objective. But let it be said in fairness that even when the instructional spirit was coming on strong, children did enter into the activity, even with gusto – though their relations with adults were constrained in a significant way by the instructional climate.

It showed up principally in the nature of the *alliance* between adult and child. Where adult directiveness was marked – as with the young volunteers at Marshall, for example, it affected not only the *play* of children, but the quality of the *conversational exchanges*. These tended to be much more impoverished in the instructional setting. They consisted of teacher telling child, and child assenting. And in the case of the shy or insecure child or the immigrant child with a shaky grasp of the language, this seemed to be self-defeating as far as development of talk was concerned.

Does a nursery make policies about such things? Probably not in so many words, and rarely at the level of decisions about how to talk to children. It is more likely that what happens at the conversational level reflects a more general attitude toward getting on with children and it is this that seemed to the observers to be part of an implicit policy that permeates a nursery. Runnymede's playgroup approach, for example, led to a lightness of touch about instruction that did not swamp good reciprocal exchanges. Wilberforce loaded itself with such a heavily instructional ideal that the adult was forced into the role of transmitter, the child that of receiver. The no-nonsensicality of Nightingale relegated the child to the end of the communication line. Osborne operated an instructional, queued, delivery system. Ironically enough, almost certainly those in charge would, if given an abstract choice, favour reciprocal exchanges as better for language development and, quite probably, they could have produced more of them had there been any planning for or even iscussion about it. But this is not what gets talked about in he all too rare staff meetings at nurseries.

Consider now the opposite of the supervised set activities, he bouts of fantasy play and make believe that children enerate on their own. Most nurseries either created or left ome time for children to play quietly in this way with little r no adult intervention. While this opportunity usually roduced play acting, make-believe and the like, the amount aried widely from one nursery to another. Some nurseries lainly provided insufficient space, time, privacy, or props wendy corner or make believe shop, for example). And one ad the impression in another that there was not so much a lisapproval of make-believe, as a sense of its being of no ccount. And sad to relate, one nursery even ruled it out nadvertently by prohibiting the children from talking to ach other in their native language, and most of them were ot fluent enough to pretend in English!

But it is not as clearcut as all that. Even with space, time, rops, and an approving adult, there are matters of adult lecorum that affect how much the children will play act, retend, and create elaborated scenarios. Two nurseries rovide interesting illustrations. In one of them, there was a very noticeable difference between two family groups – one roducing rich, high, and elaborated make-believe play, the ther not. The richer of the two had a teacher who set some limits on noise, mess, and fighting during free times, but in general let the children get on with their own activities. The other family's head was much more cooperative and entered into the make-believe – often prefacing her remarks with 'Let's all . . .'. It was not that the children in the second family did not enjoy the adult: they were lively enough with her. But it is hard to play an adult role oneself when an adult is there, and the elaborated doctor-nurse, mummy-daddy, going-shopping scenarios of the first group were rarely to be seen in the second. There are times to let children be, however zealous one might be about helping them.

Birkett, the college nursery, also had little fantasy play, in spite of being all for it in principle. The reason here was possibly different. The children were highly articulate, and many of their best exchanges among themselves took place around the table while doing something else. Their verbal fluency in exchanging news and happenings may even have pre-empted the more dramatic uses of language. Or might it have been the greater amount of television viewing at Birkett? Or even the model of academic parents more given to discursive talk than the acting out of drama? It is a subtle matter. Plainly, the children at Birkett were not suffering from verbal deprivation in any shape or form.

There is by now a sufficient body of evidence to indicate that fantasy play provides not only the opportunity for expressing and working out inner fantasies, but is a rich medium for elaborated language among children (see for instance Garvey, 1976). While the nurseries were not altogether lacking it (save in the few sad instances noted), again one had the impression that what they had got they had stumbled into rather than consciously planned for. As in our earlier discussion of the part-time care provided by play-groups, nursery schools and classes, and childminders, here too one has to note a curiously unformulated, unreflective attitude. There is, of course, the danger that *too* much adult 'consciousness' about it might take the initiative away from the children – as in the case cited – but it would surely not be amiss to help nurseries make opportunities for dramatic play and make believe.

GW have some revealing things to say about the attention or concentration of children in the day nurseries observed – although their observations cannot be quantified as in the study by SRP. They note, for one, that within a full day story time, lessons, and certain forms of set activities are often used as a means of managing and controlling the attention of children. Sometimes, to be sure, children turn off in such a regimen, but often they seem to be listening and participating. It may well be a salutary relief from having to control one's own activity and, in any case, it may be a structural necessity for a nursery open for up to ten hours a day, run by a small staff. But over and beyond that necessity, the GW notebooks contain many instances of not so much flighty attention as flighty environments full of distractions and tempting diversions. And while surely that will come as no surprise to the reader who has already met the problem in playgroup or nursery school and at the childminder's, one observation is very worth reporting. Just as SRP report that play bouts are longer when even a *non*-participating adult is nearby, so GW noted again and again that in the non-set activities children played longer and more elaborately, by themselves or in pairs or small groups, when the reassuring figure of an adult was close by. And indeed, it did not require much from the adult, sometimes nothing at all but to be there, and occasionally to offer minimal comment on some product just produced. GW comment: 'For the majority of children perhaps, an adult woman is a reassuring figure. It may merely be that, in the absence of a parent, a child needs to know that he is not abandoned or alone in order to feel it safe to give his attention fully to what he is doing.' They note how, when an adult leaves an activity table, children often look round to watch and then size up what the others are doing, as if the departure spells a new deal. Yet, 'only one nursery, Vienna Close, seemed to be aware that one could increase the likelihood of a child's remaining at an activity' either by cutting down a bit on the rate of circulation of adults from activity to activity or by reducing distractions in the room.

One final word about the children's day at the nursery before turning to the adults and their relationships with children. It has to do with the under-twos. Vienna Close, recall, saw the mother and young infant as a unit. GW report that during the first two visits no under-twos were present. When this comment was made to a senior member of staff, she laughed and said that so long as that was so, the system was working: when the mothers stayed at home with their babies it was a sign that they felt themselves able to cope. On a third visit two mothers and two staff were in the sitting room having coffee and a cigarette, while the children crawled about among the adults seated on cushions on the floor. Care for the infants was felt to be shared by *all* the adults present. A contrasting case was Nightingale where, indeed, the babies were also treated with kindness, though without much intimacy. But a routine was set, the infants well-fed and clean, and all else regarded as added work for staff – including visiting mothers. If the object of nursery care is to look after infants from families at risk, it is difficult to imagine that Nightingale is doing anything more than providing a breather for a mother under pressure – and conceivably an alienating breather at that. The question of young infants is a thorny one that relates as much to the mother as the child. Our small sample ran the gamut of contrast – one in which this issue had been carefully thought through, and one where it had been given no thought at all.

Institutional talk

From a child's eye view, obviously, the adult upon whom he is dependent is the big reality, and she can make his day or turn it to misery. But the adult's approach to looking after children, as we have noted, is strongly influenced by the institutional framework in which she finds herself. Consider some of the ways it affects her behaviour.

At Birkett, chronically but cheerfully short-handed, children were often left for quite long periods unsupervised in the TV room or even in the corridors. 'We're listening out', the supervisor would say, and in fact the children did not get into many rows. It was a small group; there was no mission to be fulfilled other than to make it possible for student mothers to get on with their work. The positive alliance was that of a group of children and a few adults who got on well together. It did not seem to the staff that they were neglecting the children – indeed they were not. Nor did the children show any sign of the clinginess that goes with the feeling of being neglected. There was mutual trust.

Wilberforce, under the pressure of a mission, created an atmosphere among staff of a contrasting kind. The children had to be got up to standard, their skills developed so that they could cope with the life that Britain has to offer its minorities. What it did was to create a high-principled but close supervision by adults of children. But where close supervision is coupled with a negative alliance it can turn close care into something sour. Take this episode as illustration:

> 'Is that yours, Dean? Did you do that? Can I see it, will you show it to me? Did you do those?'
>
> 'Tracey did them – she did them for me', replied the child innocently.
>
> The teacher reacts as though she had detected a major art forgery.
>
> 'Well, I'm not going to put *your* name on it if Tracey did it.'
>
> The child took the drawing away silently, folded it up very small and stuffed it into his pocket. The teacher turned to a colleague and said, affronted, '*She* did it for him – I saw her do it with a pencil.'

Indeed close supervision only magnifies the negative alliance until, as at Osborne Place, the very tone of voice of the staff often suggested implicitly that they expected trouble and were there to prevent it.

The alliance translates itself directly into language in so many ways – in the talk between staff as in their talk to children. It gets to the people who work in a nursery. In one of the nine nurseries (Osborne) there was virtually no conversation – neither adults nor children conversed amongst themselves or with each other. In some places, 'behaving nursery' seemed almost to preclude having conversations with the children. Within set activities the language of instruction took the place of the ordinary give-and-take of conversation. Or when the climate was chronically suspicious and controlling, exchange became curt and often inquisitional – checking up on possible trouble. GW were of the opinion that the ban on the children speaking Punjabi to each other at Osborne was supported by the (unconscious) feeling that a 'private' language is potentially subversive, as well as the conscious desire to help the children's English.

Yet most of the nurseries were not as bleak as these examples. The GW notebooks contain many instances of extended conversation, though it is unlikely that, on average, they were any more frequent than those reported in the SPR study – that is, not very frequent. But again institutional patterns operate in the ways adults reassure children, even without conversation. Paul Street (though committed in its positive alliance) was not a noticeably chatty place; people were rather weighed down with duties. But it was habitual for adults there to greet children by name as they passed, hardly even expecting the children to respond, often ruffling their hair as they passed: 'Hello Gary, All right? Hello Tracey. All right?' And in some curious way, say GW, 'this atmosphere of affection took the sting out of the clumsy way that adults in that school dealt with children's thoughtful questions'. Stressing language development as an objective of the nursery does not automatically ensure warm conversation between adult and child. At instruction-obsessed Wilberforce, the dough table was awash in talk, all of it instructional, adult originated, and designed to help the children who, at best, could ask questions to figure out what it was that the adults were instructing them to do.

Vienna Close got a high talk yield from its original decision to include parents-in-training in the nursery. Talk was not so much encouraged as simply built in by the mix of staff, volunteers, kitchen help, parents, and children. The conversation and the story telling were rich in a quite ordinary sense, requiring no more skill or expertise than talk among friends – which it was. Take an example of narrative from Vienna Close (knowing, of course, that its quality is matched by others somewhere any day). An adult with three children is looking at pictures in a book about the seaside:

> Yes, it's a crab. Do you remember how they walk?
> Sideways. Yes, sideways. I don't know any other animal
> that walks sideways! And what are these? Pincers! For

picking bits of food up and putting in their mouths. Because they eat other animals. Most animals eat other animals. You can eat crabs . . .

The passage was followed wide-eyed, and when it was done, there was a momentary tussle among the three as to which one would carry off the book for closer inspection. But what is striking is how an institutional atmosphere can stamp out such human talk.

Two principal issues, aggression and order, bring out institutional patterns with a vengeance: the first usually about fights over possessions, the second about obeying, picking up, washing up, and keeping quiet. The negative approach is simply to stop them as quickly as possible, to 'lower the boom' and issue an arbitrary decision about who is right and who is wrong. Osborne and Nightingale were on this wavelength. In neither place were the disputants 'heard' or their claims discussed. Children who squabbled often were simply branded as naughty. Angry tone to a three-year-old by a staff member at Nightingale: 'You're getting a very naughty, spiteful little girl. Now you just leave the others alone.' And to the other staff, 'You have to watch her, don't you!' Or at Marshall Day Nursery, a Matron told children that if they quarrelled any more over who should have some newly introduced toys, she'd take them out of circulation immediately. At the other pole, quarrelling is taken as a natural part of childhood, and talking it out taken as natural. Take this episode at Birkett. Some of the older boys carried their rough and tumble beyond the teacher's patience. She says:

> 'Listen, you can fight in the park if you want to, but not in here. It's too *noisy*!'
> 'But we'll get dirty in the park.' (It had been raining.)
> 'Well, that's too bad, isn't it.'

Or at Vienna Close, two boys were shouting at each other over the possession of a spade. They were watched but not stopped by a male group leader who presently said, 'I thought you two were supposed to be friends.' A moment later he put his hand on the head of the child who was trying to take the spade, telling him to wait his turn.

The 'confrontational' and 'cooperative' styles are as evident in the maintaining of order as in the handling of squabbles. Take confrontation at Nightingale:

> 'All sitting up nicely, fold your arms. . . . Do as I say or I'll put you in the corner. I'll smack you if you go on like that.'
>
> 'Who was the last to use that pipe?' (teacher continues.) 'Was that you, Simon? Did you chew the end?' (Child denies.) 'Well who did then?'
>
> 'Jane,' says the previously accused child.
>
> 'Jane, did you chew the pipe?' (She says no.) 'Well, that's not what it's for, is it? You're not supposed to chew it. Just wait till Mrs Beecham sees this.'

The cooperative style is a sharp contrast. At one nursery a teacher says, 'Joe is making such a noise I can't hear what Freddy wants', addressing the remark to both children. Or at Runnymede:

> At the beginning of one group session, the adult in charge that morning capitalized on some quietly rebellious footstamping. 'Stand up everyone who's cold! Now come on, let's have some footstamping and some hand-clapping, so's we get warm again!' There was a terrific response to this, and when the children sat down again they were quiet.

There is nothing abstract about institutional climates. They work their way into all kinds of relationships between staff and children – even to the amount and quality of talk.

Staff and support services

The largest group in day nurseries are young women in their late teens or early twenties who began on the Nursery Nurses

Education Board (NNEB) qualification training when they had finished school. They constituted 40 per cent of the staff of the nine nurseries studied by GW. A further 30 per cent had qualified in other professions such as teaching, nursing, residential child care, or teaching, but preferred to work in day nurseries. The remaining 30 per cent had either no qualifications or formal training at all, or in the case of Runnymede, the playgroup training in PPA courses. Among the untrained and unqualified were a fair scattering of younger girls who had recently left school. The bulk of the others – aside from the NNEB trained and the younger girls – were older women who had never married or who had come back to work after their children were grown. With the exception of Runnymede, young married women with nursery-aged children of their own were rarely in evidence. Runnymede and Church Road were the only ones who had made any special provision for women with young families to fit in work and family. Vienna Close, of course, had a special training arrangement for the mothers of their children, a different matter from regular employment.

There was a striking difference not only in the staff-child ratio of state and private nurseries. The former had a much more generous ratio of 1:4 in contrast to 1:7, and the qualification and training were conspicuously higher. In the state nurseries, more than four in ten of the staff were on some sort of in-service training course. Only one of the private nurseries had any in-service arrangements in force – Runnymede, which was very much part of the PPA network.

Aside from the expression of concern about whether Community Service Volunteers (the younger girls) could be left in charge of children on their own, there was not much concern expressed about staffing. Wage rates are low, and, particularly in the private nurseries, staff tenure is not long. Osborne's Organizer said her staff had been there for a 'long time', though only one in five had been there for as long as 18 months. Even though many of the places were plainly understaffed, there was not much interest in taking on volunteers, since their supervision was regarded as a chore and, perhaps, the staff did not feel themselves to be of sufficiently qualified status to manage them.

With the exception of state nurseries and those that were either related to the playgroup movement (Runnymede) or thought of themselves as having a specifically educational mission (Wilberforce), staff at day nurseries were then rather catch-as-catch can. There is little staff discussion or ideas on ways of working with children and little on the job that could be conceived of as training. To this must be added one other factor: isolation. An understaffed, under-qualified day nursery is a place full of minute-to-minute management. It is isolated from the nearby outside community just as much as from the wider outside world. It is a totally demanding, time-consuming, and long day's job. The wages are low and it is not a profession with clearcut paths to training and advancement. The Matron at Marshall knew very little about the neighbourhood in which they were located. Nightingale was immured in its hospital setting, Birkett locked into its administration tower block. The exception among the private nurseries was Runnymede, and its community setting was that of a local playgroup connected with the PPA network.

There is a DHSS/DES circular of January 1978 urging that day care facilities look to the improvement of their educational offering, suggesting particularly that there be contact between educational and health and social services in order that this may be better effected. In fact, the staff in most of the nurseries visited had very little idea of what happened to their children when they left the nursery. One aspect of their isolation is separation from the educational establishment. Of the nine nurseries visited by GW, only four had any links with the primary schools the children might later attend. And interestingly, only four had regular medical checkups for the children – and these included three of the ones who had made contact with local educational authorities. State nurseries were the ones with outside contact. In some subtle way, the financial precariousness of the private nurseries

(Wilberforce, well financed, being the exception) inhibited contact. It is difficult to reach out realistically when one is not sure that the nursery is going to make it.

One obvious way to cut down isolation is through the enlistment of parents. But this turns out not to be quite as simple as it seems. In the State nurseries, mothers' participation is principally by way of an occasional visit, and places like Paul Street, Church Road, and Vienna Close made that easy. The mothers in the private sector nurseries tended to be employed, and the attitude was more as it is at the childminders, where mothers are not usually encouraged to stay for long.

With respect to staffing, then, the picture is not encouraging. Training and qualifications in the private nurseries are distinctly lacking. Job tenure is short, hours long, and pay low. There are virtually no opportunities for nor routes to advancement and little sense of professional pride. The picture in the State nurseries is considerably better and the morale higher. But there is a notable isolation from the immediate community in which all the nurseries are located, save in a few instances. Nurseries, particularly private nurseries, also tend to be isolated from education, health and social services. In neither private nor public nurseries is there anything like a career line that would lead to greater professionalization of services, although the state nurseries do make possible further training both on the job and through courses for their people.

So the question of the climate and attitude in the nursery takes on added importance. Nurseries cannot count on a supply of helpers who have been trained or indoctrinated in nursery practice at established centres. Even State nurseries have difficulties in staffing. The largely untrained helper more than the trained one needs an implicit or explicit programme to guide her. They take on the institutional style of the place.

Some conclusions on nursery care

For all that can be said on the negative side of day nurseries,

of which more presently, it has been said that the notebooks
of the GW study have few examples of children as subdued
as those at the childminders, and this in spite of the fact that
there is a higher proportion of at-risk children to be found in
the nurseries. Perhaps the care of children in somewhat
larger groups produces less withdrawal. It is hard to know
why this is so. Even in the studies by Harlow on young
monkeys grossly abused by their parents, we noted that a
half hour a day of play with age-mates could go a long way
toward reducing the baleful effects of inadequate mothering
(Suomi and Harlow, 1975). There is obviously a lot of
difference between young monkeys in a university laboratory
and young children in an urban nursery! Yet, the fact
remains that group care seems to reduce (or childminder
care to increase) the withdrawal reaction of young children
whose mothers leave them to go to work or to go back into
community life.

With respect to the conduct of nurseries as such, I can only
reiterate what has already been said earlier. Leaving aside
for a moment any shortcomings in training and selection of
staff, there is very little question that a nursery's pervasive
style is strongly affected by the institutional objectives they
early choose or fall into. When Wilberforce commits itself to
strengthening the cognitive skills of immigrant children, it
forms their pattern to a degree that, perhaps, they could not
foresee. The style of relationship with the children reflects
lesson giving, the type of people attracted to work there is
more likely to be pedagogic, the activities more school-like
and the social life more stilted and constrained. When
Nightingale decides that its mission is looking after children
within the nursing tradition (traditionally defined) the result
is not likely to be one that tolerates the genuinely messy
impulses of children and the inbuilt variability of parents.
The three State nurseries plus Birkett and Runnymede all
opted for giving children a good social environment and a
certain supporting security.

A second implicit decision that gets taken somewhere
along the road in the early development of a day nursery

relates to 'child-centredness', if one may be permitted to use that hackneyed phrase. It describes a willingness on the part of adults to see the *child's* behaviour in terms of the *child's* intentions and aspirations, of accepting him as and where in development he is and trying to help him achieve better control, better relations, more maturity. The other extreme is judging the child in terms of his performance on a norm that is established in the world outside the child's awareness and, often, outside his comprehension. Nightingale's norms of tidiness and obedience, Osborne's centrally produced curriculum to be got through, Wilberforce's high-minded adherence to the cultivation of survival skills, and the tough teenage world imposed by the girls at Marshall – none of these made much contact with the world of children who lived within them, and one had the feeling that the children's adaptation, though not necessarily unhappy, was an adaptation to arbitrariness in the adult world.

To some extent, nurseries seek or attract staff who will behave in the light of the house style – certainly true of Vienna Close, of Runnymede; of Wilberforce. But it must surely be true too that the atmosphere sets the pattern for the individual. Church socials and choir practice produce behaviour appropriate to them and should one happen to approach them uninitiated, one very quickly picks up the cues. Day nurseries must surely be like that within limits. Yet, if one says that attitudes towards children run too deep to be affected in that way, one could surely note that regional and class accents run deep too – yet schools and colleges have been known to change them in a matter of weeks. The studies of Roger Barker (1964) on American and British secondary schools shows how school atmospheres change the behaviour of those who enter – teachers and students alike. Surely a nursery affects its staff in the same way.

Day nurseries (like part-time preschools) spend little explicit thought on what they are about, on their basic mission. Many mothers leave their children in day care because they have to: they are single parents, economically in trouble, and often deeply in trouble emotionally. There is little explicit planning about how various kinds of problems should be dealt with. Perhaps it is all at the implicit level, adults responding to the particulars of the individual child's problems. The observations certainly do not suggest that this is widespread – though a few day nurseries are sensitive in just this way.

The general conclusions reached by the GW study are worth pausing over. Their first one concerns the importance of explicitness on the part of parent and nursery as to the 'contract' for caring for a child – with both sides acknowledging more fully *why* the child needs to be looked after. Where the mother is in desperate need, has been referred through a social worker, and where the nursery has a policy designed to care for children in this plight, explicitness is built into the arrangement. The issue is then, so to speak, to keep accounts current and communication going. And as we saw in the study of the minders, that is not easy. But often, the situation is not desperate and there is often self-deception as to the role the nursery is playing and what it is that the mother can expect. GW are of the view that the heavy-handed emphasis on set activities and instruction found in so many nurseries, particularly the private ones, is a way in which nurseries respond to the ambiguity of their role. *That*, at least, is 'educational', different from what the child would get if at home, and therefore a justification for day care in the absence of desperate need on the part of the parent.

Their second point is an extension of the first. A child away from home for the full day, they feel, cannot be subjected to a full day of educational emphasis. The pre-school child, away from home for the day, simply has too many emotional and social needs to be fulfilled to be educated all day long either in the interest of developing survival skills as a minority child or even learning how to behave and be obedient. This is not to say that there should be little emphasis on cognitive development, but that all should be subordinated to the child's emotional security and development. 'What we are saying is that the two-, three-, and four-year-old must be enabled to proceed at his own pace within a framework whose *primary* concern is with the satisfaction of his emotional and social needs. Only then can the goals of cognitive growth be pursued with justification and responded to with enthusiasm.' One crucial part of solving this problem is to reduce the sharpness of the distinction between 'play' and 'work' – *not* to be mindful only of the latter and unresponsive to the former.

And finally, a commitment to the child as he is, seeking his own expression and pursuing his goals – rather than a judge-mental approach in terms of adult norms – is the best assurance of the child's basic security in the nursery. It often goes hand in hand with a more democratic and collegial relation between the people who must look after the child there. The two, a respect for children's problems *and* colle-gial mutual respect in the staff, are built into the *modus vivendi* of the *nursery* at the time the nursery is established. It is worth a long pause for reflection at the very start to make clear just what ends people have in mind in coming together to set up a nursery altogether.

In the main, if I may add to the GW conclusions, there has been little thought given to what private nurseries are for, and little guidance given to them by social services or education departments. Both these lack appropriate staff to give counsel and are too understaffed and overstretched to help much. The State-supported nurseries of Greater Lon-don, judging at least from the handful studied, seem to be doing better, are less isolated and more open to training and guidance. But there are precious few of them.

Banal though the remark may seem, it is hard not to say at the end of this preliminary study of London day nurseries, that we still know relatively little about them, about how best to run them or to train people to do so. Had there been the expected expansion in nursery education promised in 1972, it is not likely that the expansion would automatically have improved practice. At the very least, we shall have to find out far more of what is required by a child in full day care whose mother wishes to – or must – work, or who has fallen victim to the pressures of living in modern society. Ironically, there is time now to explore these matters in some detail before any nursery expansion can be envisaged.

In fact our exploration turned up some models. The cooperative, parent-training plan of Vienna Close is one such. The extended, all-day playgroup with parent volunteers at Runnymede is another. The single-purpose compensatory education model of Wilberforce (after Bereiter and Engelman) is yet another (although GW feel it is too rigidly educational too early in the life of the child). Nightingale and Osborne speak to the difficulties of company nurseries. Church Road and Paul Street serve a community even if they are not particularly outstanding with the children. They are sound State nurseries, subject to improvement. Marshall is that rather sad spectacle of a well meaning private day nursery so short of resources that it must take on unqualified staff who defeat its own purpose. The nurseries studied are a British mix of vision, pragmatism, and muddling. If there were one sector of British preschool care that would benefit from the clearer enunciation of a policy toward young children in Britain, it would be the day nursery sector, for that is where – given the whole long day – it would be most immediately felt.

It must be said finally that there is no *reason of merit* that compels the recommendation that day nurseries *as they now operate* should be greatly increased in number. Expansion should be highly selective and geared to developing models for later use, when the economic climate can support a larger scale expansion of services. Plainly, more are needed. But day nurseries that are worth the investment require trained staff and training opportunities on the job. They need support from and connection with the community. They need a clearer sense of their function than most of them seem to have. They require more connection with the educational system and with social services. And finally, they should be conceived in terms of their relation to the other forms of care available, a matter for the following chapter.

One of the most critical problems in any expansion,

selective or general, is the formulation of more explicit plans about the function of day nurseries. Perhaps I have already harped enough on this theme – not only in this chapter, but in the two preceding ones. In the case of the day nursery, locked into a full day's operation, the matter takes on even greater importance than for part-time preschools and for minders. Critical decisions about what a day nursery should be for and how it should go about its business of care have, as we have seen in this chapter, had an enormous effect on later practice. I can think of few happy by-products of the present freeze on spending for day nurseries. Yet one such might be to put limited resources into a relatively few model day nurseries and the support systems that are needed. Some of these might surely be based on the volunteer, rota concept of the full-day playgroup. Others might take the form of family-centred units, where the intake is principally for at-risk children. Still others might be based on more intensive study of various day-care facilities that have come into being around Britain to look after the children of mothers at work or who are in full-time study. We are in a period of serious retrenchment economically, to be sure, but it could be a period for exploring possibilities for the future. It is unlikely for the next half decade that Britain will be able to meet the day-care needs of working mothers or of families in trouble through the expensive alternative of full-day State-supported nurseries. But it would be a grave error not to invest in research and in pilot projects that look towards a future in which such nurseries may again be a possibility of choice in the provision of care.

8

Appraisals and proposals

Two large questions pose themselves at the end of this inquiry. Is there sufficient preschool provision – in quality and quantity – to ensure a competent next generation? And is there the means in Britain for developing policies about such a question that are at once rational, compassionate, and economically viable? Neither question can be answered with unequivocal certainty, yet we have now enough information in hand to inform our reflections and even to suggest some conclusions.

There is no better place to start than with the 1978 Report of the Central Policy Review Staff (the Cabinet 'think tank') on *Services for Young Children with Working Mothers*. Both its analysis of the problems of children under five and its recommendations, though addressed to the problems of working mothers and their children, bear on the larger issues of a national policy for young children. After sifting the evidence on needs and resources, the Report concludes with the question of whether 'the government's existing role is sufficient, given the intrinsic importance of ensuring that young children in our society have adequate attention paid to their needs'. They single out four aspects of existing services that are inadequate:

(a) There is a lack of direction and no clear priorities as to the ways in which services should progress.

(b) There is confusion in the administration of services for children under five. The provision of services is fragmented and responsibility is divided.

(c) The consequences of the present situation for the children and their parents are both unjust and inequitable. There is a serious lost opportunity for preventative work at an early stage.

(d) It is widely recognized that children benefit from some education and care outside their homes between the ages of three and five. A substantial number of children are denied this benefit because adequate provision is not available.

How inadequate the provision is can be summed up in what is presented as one of the two main findings of this careful study:

> In Great Britain there are some 900,000 children under five whose mothers have a job; the government provides or controls full- and part-time day care for about 120,000 children in day nurseries and with childminders.

Or more bluntly still,

> . . . there are over three quarters of a million children under 5 whose mothers work and who have at present no access to local authority day nurseries or child minder provision.

No surprise then that the survey commissioned by the DHSS (Bone, 1977) reports that while a third of *all* parents of children under five feel they need no provision, that they can manage on their own, and another third have found the provision they want, there remains a third who have not been able to find the provision they need for their children. These figures (based as they are on children from birth to five) indicate that far *more* than a third are unserved, and for two reasons. In the first place, if one examines the responses of the parents of threes and fours, the proportion of those who say they have not found provisions they feel are adequate rises to two thirds. And, secondly, it is true of most human needs, that supply creates demand; the provision of more and better services for preschool children would increase the demand among parents for such services.

Nor does the bare provision of services tell the whole story. For present services are felt by parents to be, in the stark words of the CPRS Report, 'inadequate, and in many cases seriously so'. Whether considered quantitatively or qualitatively, Great Britain has seriously fallen behind in the provision of care for its under-fives. Dissatisfaction is general among parents whether or not the mother works, strikingly so among the families of three- and four-year-olds but also to a considerable extent even among families with younger children. The emergence of a playgroup movement in the voluntary sector has relieved some of the demand for part-time places, but parents are by no means satisfied either with the quantity or the quality of provisions available to their children on a full-time basis.

Our task in the preceding chapters has been mainly to consider the quality of care made available by the different forms of provision. And while most of the conclusions in this final chapter relate to quality, it is impossible to ignore the question of quantity. Indeed, one of the principal recommendations of the 1978 CPRS Report is for 'a substantial change in present policies, requiring a change in emphasis from expensive services for a small number to a reasonable service for a much larger number. The shift in emphasis from professionally staffed (and expensive) nursery schools to somewhat less expensive nursery classes and to strikingly less expensive playgroups has been a *de facto* policy decision in just that direction precipitated by the failure, or inability, of central government and of local authorities to finance the expansion of nursery schools of the classical type. Fortunately the playgroup movement took up the slack, else Britain today would be much worse off and, indeed, would be pondering the quantity-quality dilemma even more agonizingly than it is.

Before turning then to issues of quality and how quality may be improved, it is crucial to consider the matter of places provided and how quantity and quality interact.

Take first the needs of children whose mothers have jobs – the 700,000 whose mothers work less than 30 hours a week and the 200,000 children of full-time working mothers. The CPRS Report recommends strongly as a general policy that plans for expansion be based upon an enlargement and enrichment of provisions now in being, and that (along with the Report's emphasis upon flexibility) is surely a realistic approach. The basic recommendation is that day nursery care and nursery education should be combined or linked whenever possible, and that this should be accomplished by two relatively low-cost expedients. The first is to use 'more intensively the facilities of the nursery schools', noting that 'recent experiments have shown that at comparatively little cost the nursery school session could be extended for another two or three hours until parents are able to come and collect their children'. The second is to use spare classroom facility as it becomes available with the decline in school populations for nursery classes – thereby saving considerably in capital outlay for expansion. I think both of these suggestions admirable. Indeed, the establishment of 'combined centres' would have the effect of enriching the educational input into day nurseries. This is indeed what has happened in the few combined centres that have been studied by Elsa Ferri at the National Children's Bureau, and while (as noted in Chapter 2) combining the two types of service produces some staff problems (given the different histories of the caring and educational professions) the results have been favourable. Certainly the French experience in extending nursery school hours to accommodate working mothers has been effective and, after all, the full-day nursery school is standard practice not only in many Western countries, but in virtually all the countries of Eastern Europe. Little doubt too that combined centres would stimulate a badly needed dialogue locally and in Whitehall between social services and education. In considering London day nurseries, recall, it was very apparent that they were isolated from outside influences – particularly from educational authorities.

But there are two places, it seems to me, where the CPRS Report either fails to grasp an opportunity or takes hold of an available but chancy one with insufficient caution. One opportunity is the use of the extended day playgroup, a successful example of which we visited in Chapter 7, the Runnymede Playgroup. It ran by the expedient of extending its daily session till about 4.00 p.m. yet some of the mothers who worked part-time were able to help out. Is there a possible model here? The Report quite rightly notes that most employed mothers work between 20 and 30 hours a week. Surely (and with urging from the Department of Employment) it would be possible to arrange those hours to make it possible for mothers to have a job *and* to take a hand in arrangements for looking after their children. There is surely a lack of imagination in present working hours for employed mothers with young children. It is not so much a matter of realistic requirements at work as an attitude, and neither employers nor child care organizations seem to have faced the problem openly and intelligently. There are also some doctrinaire views that get in the way of realism. There is, for example, considerable resistance within the major voluntary association, the PPA, to an expansion of play-groups with extended hours or other modifications suited to working mothers. The PPA is decentralized, however, and has grown by accommodating itself flexibly to new needs as they arise locally. There would be secondary gains for working mothers in such playgroup arrangements. Working mothers have much to share and if, indeed, the playgroup movement is an expression of the 'mature woman's movement' (as I tried earlier to argue), the addition of working members could only be a bonus. There is little reason to believe that the Runnymede Playgroup was deliv-ering any less adequate a service than most of the other centres discussed in Chapter 7. The entry into full day care by a lively playgroup movement could go a long way towards improving the training for day nurseries, and increasing the pool of people available for staffing them.

More worrisome is the risky proposal in the CPRS Report for the use of childminders as a means of taking up slack in full-day provision. The Report begins with proper caution by admitting that 'Bad childminding can have social consequences that are both difficult and expensive to try to set right, and the present service is inadequate and piecemeal.' Is it enough to urge that childminders be got to register with local authorities and given help and support? Or that they should 'be regarded as colleagues by professional workers in the field' when in fact they do not regard themselves in any sense as professionals or as the colleagues of professionals? It is somewhat empty to urge local authorities 'to develop schemes for childminders', when in fact, very few local authorities have been able to make any progress in doing so. I think it would be far more prudent to conclude – on the basis of the Bryant, Harris, and Newton study in our Project, the Petrie and Mayall study at the Thomas Coram Research Unit in London, and Brian Jackson's recent report – that childminding should *not* be expanded until, in the words of the TUC Report, it is re-examined and reorganized root and branch. Childminding is a risky form of care even with initially sympathetic and kindly and conventionally competent minders and should not be expanded without some reliable means of spotting early on which children fail to thrive in such care. One proposal for an early warning system has already been made (Chapter 6) and we shall return to it again on a later page. Childminding may one day be an investment in 'low cost realism', but that day has not yet come and will not come until present, widespread doubts about it are resolved. But there are many ways in which childminders could be used as *aides* to supplement extended hour nursery schools, playgroups, or day nurseries. In the present combined centres, for example, there may be a place for minders to take up the hour or two between more formal school-closing and the time when mothers finish their day's work. The dilemma of school holidays, with children out of nursery school but mothers at work, could be managed by small groups from extended nurseries and playgroups going to a minder who had already come to know them in the school or playgroup setting. In so far as minders became an ancillary service to playgroups, nurseries, and day-care centres, the problems that stem from the domestic isolation of the childminders might be reduced. And certainly there would, under these circumstances, be a greatly enhanced opportunity to monitor for any of the bad effects of minding reported in Chapter 6.

As for recommendations about the quantity of *part-time* nursery education, it is difficult to know what is realistic, at least financially. There is a great deal to be said in support of the CPRS recommendation to provide reasonable care for many rather than expensive care for a few. The findings reported in Chapter 5 suggest that there is not enough difference between present nursery school care and play-group care to justify a five- to ten-fold difference in capital outlay for the two and a nearly four-fold difference in running costs (cf. CPRS Report, p.27f). Nursery schools represent an enormous initial capital investment (roughly £910 per place provided at 1976 prices) whereas playgroups often make do with none at all by using spare capacity in church halls and the like. The running cost differential of £650 per place for nursery schools versus about £200 for playgroups may even obscure a more serious inequity. The former draws almost exclusively on public funds; the latter on fees from individual parents. The real differential, then, must take into account that parents who lay out £200 per year to send a child to a playgroup are also paying the taxes that raise the £260,000,000 (at 1976 levels) to send other people's children to free nursery schools and day nurseries. If there are no other facilities available to them, it cannot be said that they are being made to pay more for choosing private care. They simply have no choice. Just as it would seem to make sense to increase full-day care by extending the hours of nursery schools and classes, and locating them in the classrooms made available by the drop in the birth rate, so would it make sense to increase part-time nursery educa-tion by increasing public support of playgroups to encourage their further development – quantitatively and qualitatively. However remarkable the rise of playgroups may be as a social phenomenon, it is still the case that they vary widely in their quality. There are some that are lively and imaginative;

others are dull and routine and could be improved by more training and better resources. In so far as half a million children are being catered for by playgroups, it seems only sensible to invest resources to improve their quality – not by coercive standards, which would threaten their voluntary nature, but by the offer of help and encouragement.

It is difficult to judge in such uncertain economic and political times how much and in what ways to fill the dangerous gap between need and supply in the amount of full and part time care needed in Great Britain. Doubtless it is true, as CPRS say, that 'the capacity of the system to develop without additional resources is small'. The CPRS proposal of £150,000,000 a year over five years surely cannot prime the pump sufficiently to produce three quarters of a million places – even if the present Conservative Government or a later Labour Government were willing to make the investment. But such earmarked grants would surely be a healthy stimulant and a morale booster. It is certainly worth the try, particularly if, as recommended, support is given in response to the submission of reasoned local proposals for expansion. A figure of £300,000,000 would be far more realistic.

That much said, consider now the question of the *nature* and *quality* of the forms of care available and what steps might reasonably be taken better to fit provision to need. In discussing issues of this order, I am not proposing expensive care for the few in preference to reasonable care for the many. The spirit of the inquiry, rather, is how to improve *any* of the forms of care available and how to help them better to fill the needs for which they were designed.

Commonsense and expert opinion on the effects of early care both demand that we look at quality. A policy for expansion that failed to do so would continue to waste effort and money and could, indeed, multiply troubles. Quality education and care matter at every age in a child's educational career – whether in preschool (Hohmann, Banet, and Weikart, 1979) or at the secondary level (Rutter *et al.*, 1979). The effects of early educational opportunities do not wash out later, although they can be obliterated by subsequent alienation. Weikart's High/Scope Project followed their preschoolers through secondary school and into employment. After a decade and a half, the group that had received quality preschooling were far ahead of their unschooled control mates in school achievement, in school completion, in number employed and quality of jobs held – and ahead in IQ as well.

Can these results be generalized from the socio-economically less privileged child who is being given a 'head start' against bad odds to the ordinary child in a preschool, or at a minder's, or in a playgroup? Wherever the question has been put directly to test – and the Bennett (1976) and the Rutter study just cited are relevant – it has turned out to be the case that quality education has good effects and can, indeed, overcome earlier poor starts. It is a bald and unvarnished conclusion as stated, for we also know that there are circumstances that are severe enough to obliterate any advantages that might accrue from the best schooling. Earlier studies (like Jencks' in 1972) that purported to show that schooling and its quality mattered little by comparison with social class have not held up to close scrutiny. Their results were consistently flawed by a failure to follow the *same* children over time, children from different social classes. When such follow-up is available, quality of schooling *does* matter.

Does quality in education matter more or less in the early years? There are obviously second chances later in life, and a failure to make friends in playgroup or to master mathematics games in nursery school does not condemn a child thereafter to the life of a social isolate or to the fate of innumeracy. Human childhood, more than that of other species, is marked by extraordinary plasticity. But just as plainly, there are certain early attitudes and skills upon which later ones must be built. A fear of failure, developed early, will inhibit the confident use of mind later. Resistance to adults, early established, is not easily shed. An uncertain reader cannot be as readily tempted by the lure of literature.

The earlier a skill can be mastered without tears and sacrifice of other values, the more will it contribute to a child's life and form the basis for other skills. And the earlier in life an educational setback is encountered the more important to set it right as quickly as possible before it affects the later mastery of skills that are based upon it. It is easier to set it right earlier than later, before failure becomes incorporated in an attitude.]

So what may we say about the quality of the preschool provision that is now available? It is better, perhaps, to begin where matters appear to be worst – in full-day care, and particularly at the minder's.

Our Project's study – conducted by Bryant, Harris, and Newton – concluded that childminding in its present form creates problems for at least a third of children in such care, and for possibly as many as a half. The 'quality' of the minder, her degree of concern for children, and the setting in which she works, help surprisingly little, though we know that when the setting is less fortunate and the quality of care less good than in Oxfordshire, the degree of difficulty increases. That much is revealed by the studies of Petrie and Mayall in Inner London, and from the Jacksons' work. But improving the setting, choosing qualified minders, and so on, do not solve the problem of children in such care. The heart of the problem, as it emerged in Oxfordshire, appears to be the discontinuity between home and the minder's for the child, and the lack of adequate communication between minder and mother. The incidence of 'quiet' or mildly depressed children at the competent and well-placed minders' is too great to overlook and it has been remarked too often to be adventitious. It can be said statistically that the greater the tension and trouble in the home of the child, the more likely is such depressed behaviour to appear at the minder's, whatever her qualifications or setting. The minder does not see herself as a professional in any way, and certainly not as an amateur psychiatrist. Since the minder does not regard it as part of her job to 'pry' into the child's home life and since it appears to be the rare mother who shares her personal troubles with her minder, the child's problems are not faced by either. The problems probably lie in the child being put into minding without all parties being explicit and open about the feelings this creates. However much one would want it to be otherwise, the minder's, for many children, is not a home away from home (however homelike it is by conventional standards) but an empty time separated from home. In most instances there appears little the minder can do about that – save to let the child be. Minders, the Bryant, Harris, and Newton study shows, are a decidedly domestic lot. And while in the crowded confines of Inner London they may leave their charges understimulated in bare surroundings, even when there are toys and gardens available, as in Oxfordshire, the withdrawn children constitute a very substantial minority.

With neither social services nor health visitors readily available, the minder has nowhere to turn when she is concerned about a child. The mother, often escaping from a sense of being trapped inside the four walls of the home and cut off from the adult world, may often be too ready to turn a somewhat blind eye so long as the child's problems take the form of quietness. Two major studies – ours and Petrie and Mayall's – have both pointed to this syndrome, if one may use so drastic a term. *Some* children, perhaps even the *majority* of children, fare well at the minder's. The issue, rather, is what can be done to help the substantial minority who do *not*.

In an earlier chapter (page 130) it was suggested that there be established a system of visiting minders, drawn from among experienced minders and operating under an association of childminders. They could provide counsel to individual minders and also maintain a working contact with a childminding team operating regionally – a team composed of the relevant specialities, including psychiatry. Most of the staff needed for such teams are already in being. At very least (for there are many positive things that these visitors could do to help minders), such a network could serve to spot children who are failing to thrive in minding and help their parents to seek professional advice. In general, it has been found that those least likely to thrive are those children from homes in trouble, where professional help is most likely to be needed.

But in general, the findings of research on childminding surely suggest that great caution should be exercised in expanding this form of service. A careful re-examination of standards of minding care is needed – particularly in urban areas. The Jackson and the Petrie and Mayall studies do not support the hope that minding might provide a home away from home. The initial concern about backstreet minders may not be fully justified, but there is still enough evidence of bleakness in the care presently provided to justify a close and thorough examination.

What of day nurseries? A close look at nine of them in Greater London showed them varying from a stiffly inadequate, commercially-run factory crèche to one that by any standards would have to be regarded as a model in dealing not only with children, but with their at-risk families to whom the children would have eventually to return. They vary widely indeed. The State-run nurseries seem to do better both from the point of view of quality and continuity of staff and contact with supporting services, though they are often unable or unwilling to take family problems into account in their care. They serve, rather, as havens away from home for children with troubled families (the chief source of children in such full-day care). Some of the privately run nurseries do little indeed by way of providing a stimulating experience; their educational activities are unimaginative, and the children's play uninspired. Staff are not well trained and turnover is high. In most of the day nurseries observed, there was little rationale in what was done, little consciousness of the function to be served. This was sometimes compensated by a warm and human atmosphere in which staff and children took pleasure in each other's company. Some nurseries, however, had a moralistic, confrontational style, that made for a stand-off between adults and children.

It was strikingly the case that almost all the private-sector nurseries operated in isolation – in isolation from school services related to the later lives of their children, from medical authorities, and indeed from the broader community of parents and professionals who concern themselves with care. There was no source of guidance to which they turned. Each seemed preoccupied with its daily problems and rarely looked outward for ideas about practice. In consequence (with some exceptions, of course) their practices expressed a range of rather conventional attitudes towards the young – moral-punitive, *laissez-faire*, or even busily pedagogic. Day nurseries, with few exceptions, reflect little and discuss even less what they are doing and why. For all that, the more active, peer-related existence of children in day nurseries seems to keep them from falling into the 'quietness' of mild depression found reported at minders – in spite of the fact that many of them come from disturbed homes.

Looking at the two forms of provision, day nurseries and childminders, several differences strike me. The first is in social atmosphere. By dint of sheer numbers, the day nursery is bound to be a peer group: there are lots of other children about who are sharing the same situation, the same plight. The day nursery is in no sense a simulation of home, and however much it may be organized in terms of small family groups to assure intimacy (a method of managing that seems to pay off well for children and staff alike), it is still child centred and organized for children away from home. Little question that this creates some problems of adjustment, yet it is a distinctively different setting from home and demands from the child a different approach to getting on. If the day nursery manages to create an atmosphere of collaboration between children and staff, it can be (as we have seen) a highly congenial setting. At its worst, a day nursery with a confrontational style and a moralistic approach can be an unhappy place, although even there there is always the possibility of compensation in the company of selected peers.

The childminder's, in contrast, is a home situation in which the child is living under the umbrella of daily domesticity. At its best, it is in effect a *second* home in which the child feels in a familiar, protected and undemanding situation. But the crucial factor controlling whether the child adjusts to such a home away from home is how things are going at home itself. If his own home is a source of anxiety and tension exacerbated by anxieties about the stability of his emotional ties there, a minder's home away from home may be neither a relief from nor a compensation for troubles at his own. Even at the kindliest minder's, we know from the Oxfordshire study, the troubled child may simply withdraw and go inwards. There will be none of the demands either of a peer group or of a round of regular activity to bring him out of it. For some children even the best minding situation works poorly and no satisfactory relationship develops between minder and child for the poignant reason that no woman, minder or not, can come closer to a child than a child will let her – unless some unusual intervention occurs that redefines the minding situation and its relationship to the home, and that requires a closer collaboration between mother and minder than ordinarily prevails.

It is worth an aside to comment on the role of the peer group in early childhood as a source of security and comfort. It has always been a part of common sense that children after about two and a half take comfort in and are cheered into action by the presence of their peers and older children as well. What brought this commonsense matter more forcibly to the attention of students of development was the finding reported by Suomi and Harlow (1975) that young monkeys, raised away from their mothers on a terry-cloth 'dummy mother' to which they could cling and get a feed were spared many of the most devastating effects produced by such separation if they were allowed access to a group of age mates for as little as 20 minutes a day. Their social, intellectual, and emotional development was far less retarded than among control animals who were totally isolated. And in more natural setting among higher primates in the wild, chimpanzees, Goodall's studies (1971) have similarly shown the importance of the peer group in development. To this add human studies on how language is acquired in the world's cultures: McNeill and McNeill (undated) have found that in *most* extant societies, the principle source of language learning was other children. We may, in our society of the nuclear family, be underestimating the role of peers. Studies of the Israel *Kibbutz* (by M. E. and A. G. Spiro, and others, 1975) underline how easy and satisfactory is the transition for the child from his peer group to his parents once an expectancy of regular alternation is established. That expectancy seems to create few difficulties for the child. No surprise then that there has been a generation of satisfactory experience of regular day nursery attendance in the Socialist countries of Eastern Europe and the democracies of the West.

All of which is certainly not to imply that childminding is intrinsically a poorer system than day nurseries. Many children thrive at the minder's. The troublesome issue is how to cope with the children who do *not*, and both common sense and professional judgement argue for removing them if they are adjusting badly. Or, more wisely, keeping the child who has troubles at home from getting *into* a minding situation. For him, it is more than likely that a day nursery (of good quality) is indicated. Even more patently indicated in such instances is a support system that will help the troubled family as well. And here one can do no better than to point to the unfulfilled recommendation to that effect of the Finer and the Court Reports.

But it is an error to suppose that all day nurseries or even *most* day nurseries are of the quality needed. The Garland and White study of nine London day nurseries points to enormous variety and some very poor quality. The educational input in many day nurseries, as we have noted, is unimaginative and their isolation from other sources of practice is marked. Particularly where threes and fours are concerned, the challenge and opportunity offered is below that of many nursery schools and playgroups. In the light of all this, the proposal made by the Central Policy Review Staff in their 1978 Report on services for children seems very attractive: to extend the hours of nursery schools so that they may be converted into combined nursery schools and day nurseries. Where it has been tried in Britain, as already stated, it has proved a good arrangement, and it is after all the accepted standard in most other countries. There is every reason (as noted earlier in this chapter as well) to provide more opportunity for playgroups to extend their hours particularly to accommodate the children of mothers who work part-time – the great bulk of the female labour force with children of preschool age.

Can one answer realistically the question whether, for full day care, the day nursery or the childminder is better? Part of the answer is clear enough: for the child with troubles at home, good day nurseries are to be preferred. As for other children, I think the answer can only be found by a searching examination of minding, particularly with a view to encouraging minders themselves, in association, to explore ways of improving their service through the kinds of support networks mentioned earlier. It would be foolish to imagine that the task of improving childminding services will be easy – for the reasons explored in Chapter 6. Most minders, at present, do not see their jobs as involving professional skills, and a good part of the task will be to make them conscious of the fact that such skills *are* involved, and that such skills are *attainable*. To those who say that such a profound change in attitude is impossible, the best answer is an historical one. Kindergartens and nursery schools, after all, are new on the scene in an historical sense and their operation is now seen as involving professional skills. A start was made by a small nucleus of dedicated practitioners of the 'nursery movement'. What is needed now is a start of a 'minders' movement' and that seems to be on its way.

As to the quality of the three main forms of part-time provision – nursery school, nursery classes, and playgroups – it is admittedly difficult to find an appropriate yardstick by which to judge. Parents send children for a variety of reasons. Often they simply 'know it is good for them'. Doubtless, there are personal needs as well: to get some relief from child care. More articulate parents cite the

desirability of getting children 'weaned' from home in preparation for later attendance at schoool, of helping them learn
to play with their peers, of giving them a wider scope for
learning how to communicate, and of giving them a start in
'pre-' subjects – pre-mathematics, pre-reading, and the like.
Does it succeed at all these things? If the quality is high
enough, probably yes. 'Is it high enough?' Not an easy
question to answer simply, for it depends on aspirations and
resources. There are doubtless some exaggerated claims, for
example, about playgroups and nursery schools aiding language learning. And they do in their way. Yet a recent study by
Barbara Tizard (1979) shows that the quality of mother-child
talk at home, built on shared topics and presuppositions, is
richer and more finely tuned than language in nursery
school. But it is also important to learn to talk with stran-
gers – age mates and teachers. Is there enough opportunity
for *that*? On balance, while the research shows that nursery
schools and playgroups both do produce improvements in
linguistic, social, intellectual, and emotional maturity (the
more so the higher the quality) there is also plenty of room
for improvement.

A child in a preschool group expresses his powers to the
full – imaginative, practical, whatever – when he is attracted
to and able to concentrate upon the tasks he undertakes.

What produces the kind of concentration that yields the
fullest and richest elaboration of play? The studies carried
out in Oxfordshire point to a series of conditions, all of which
can be readily improved. They relate to such relatively
mundane matters as curriculum, the social structure of the
children at school, the role of staff, and the models of play
the school establishes in the minds of children through group
activity.

Where curriculum is concerned, the richest, most elaborated and most extended play occurs with materials that can
be structured by the child in terms of the observable properties of the material. These are activities in which a clear
relation can be seen between means and ends, a relation that
the child can see on his own and without the intervention of a

teacher or play leader – construction activities, puzzles, school-like games, pretend play with small toys, and so forth. Children play more elaborately and for longer and more concentrated bouts with such materials than with less structured materials such as clay, water, sand, dough, and finger paints. It is not a question of structured versus unstructured materials. Rather the problem is to give children a real opportunity and challenge to discover to the full their powers of concentration. A curriculum does not have to include *only* such challenges (any more than a meal should have only a meat course!) but it will fail to stimulate a child to his full powers if it includes too few.

Young children play longer and better when they operate in pairs than when they are in larger groups where distraction and temptations become unmanageable. The intimacy of shared activity in a pair is a powerful stimulus and support for play and it is the rare nursery school or playgroup that provides sufficient opportunity for such undistracted pair-play. The presence of an adult nearby, easily available to the child for confirmation or reassurance but not managing, similarly improves the quality of play – partly by buffering against distraction and partly by the subtle process of being there for the odd confirming comment as needed. It will come as no surprise, then, that playgroups and nursery schools with more staff produce more elaborated free play among their children.

Schools in which there are more than a bare minimum of group activities involving structured and intellectually demanding play promote more elaborated play among the children when they are back on their own, doing their own thing. Whether the children are getting a message about what is the thing to do or whether they are learning skills or whether they only need a small amount of encouragement to get on with what they want to do really, we do not know. Whatever it is, it appears to enrich spontaneous play.

There seems to be, then, an untapped capacity for elaborated play that is not fully enough engaged by most playgroups and nursery schools. Distraction, insufficient chance to work closely with another single child, unchallenging materials, the absence of 'buffering' adults on the staff, an absence of exemplifying activities – all of these seem to keep this capacity from expressing itself fully and in a fashion to help in the cultivation of mind. One gets the impression, observing nursery schools and playgroups, that they are often unclear and at cross purposes about what they are trying to do. They attempt to serve so many functions that (though they serve some of them very well for some children) they fail to enlist to the full the growing intellectual energies and skills of the three- and four-year-olds whom they principally serve.

The cultivation of speech and language is usually taken as another important function of nursery schools and playgroups. Do they provide as much opportunity for this as they could or should? In some respects, yes. For the less structured activities one frequently finds do provide opportunity for more talking. But it is not often the kind of connected talk that brings out the child's full linguistic capacities. The rare privacy of a pair of children playing undistracted at a pretend game produces rich connected conversation – and the opportunity is not often available in the hurly-burly of the average nursery school or playgroup. And perhaps the best inspiration to prolonged and connected conversation is a teacher joining a small group of children as a *participant in the play*. But the chores of managing the children in playgroups and nursery schools (as they are now run) make participation by teachers an altogether rare event. Yet, teachers who observed and discussed a recording of their own interactions with children learned to contain their managerial role and to take a much more active and richer part in conversation with their children. The sooner findings of this order work their way into teacher training, the better off teachers and children will be.

These studies surely suggest that there is ample room for more planning and improvement in the quality of playgroups and nursery schools and classes. As between them, there is little to choose in terms of which generates more concentrated play, and more prolonged connected conversation. We have already commented on the cost of the three provisions – with nursery schools the most expensive by far in capital outlay and in running costs and playgroups by far the cheapest in both respects. There is always discussion in progress on the relative merits or the alternative uses of these three forms of part-time preschool provision. Does the present inquiry add anything to that discussion?

The first thing to be said is that our study of the three types of provision in Oxfordshire does not in any sense constitute a complete evaluation of the different ways of organizing part-time preschool education. Only one county was studied. And our measures of elaborated play, connected conversation, and so on, do not constitute the only reasonable yardsticks by which worth can be assessed. Nor have we carried out follow-up studies to see how children fared in school or in the community later. Nonetheless, it is possible to make some comments that may be helpful.

The first is that labels tell little. It is not easy to distinguish a playgroup from a nursery school from a nursery class except by the sign on the door. The play of the children is much alike in all three. As noted in Chapter 5, there are far better predictive indices than these labels. The number of staff (paid or unpaid) matters more than the label – with its associated message concerning capital outlay, running cost, or even statutory status – provided the staff is adequately prepared and relations between children and staff are happy. The form of curriculum and the mode of organizing the day matter greatly – and there is much overlap between the three types of preschool provision. There can be little doubt that the training now given playgroup leaders has provided Britain with a surprisingly large pool of good supervisors and 'teachers' for preschools and at astonishingly small public cost. I put 'teachers' in inverted commas because the Pre-school Playgroup Association tends to define its role not as teaching but as leading the children in play, but since that is the principal teaching business of the preschool, I take the point as a semantic one. In the balance between 'expensive care for the few' versus 'reasonable care for the many', the playgroup movement has surely tipped the scales towards the latter.

One point needs to be added. The more intensive and longer training of nursery school teachers prepares them, I believe, not only for what they do but for more demanding work than many of them are now called upon to do. And this, I believe, gives more weight to the proposal of the Central Policy Review Staff to combine the function of nursery schools and day nurseries by extending the hours of the former so that they can also accommodate the latter. The nursery schools, moreover, represent a very considerable investment of educational funds – more than £175 million pounds of public funds annually for running costs, leaving aside the cost of training staff and providing capital outlay. Rather than phasing them out – as was proposed in Oxfordshire as our study was reaching its end – it would be far more economical to use them and their expert staffs as the experimental growing edge, so to speak, for developing new and better provisions for meeting the new child-care needs of a changing Britain. It is from them as a specialist group that one might reasonably solicit new ideas for future care. One idea has already been proposed: the combined centre.

Given this special function, it would be more appropriate to finance such experimental nursery enterprises from earmarked national funds allocated for this purpose rather than finance them, as now, from Rate Support Grants urgently needed for local services. It is a tiny investment but crucial for the future. It would keep alive a sense of venture and exploration in the most highly trained segment of the preschool community. Accordingly, grants should be awarded on merit and in response to concrete proposals. The presence of such a programme of nursery support should include a research and development component on the early years sponsored by research councils, universities, polytechnics, and training colleges. The opportunity is too great to pass by and need justifies the small cost involved.

As for playgroups, the first thing that must be said is that they have served a major and crucial role in filling the gap in the part time care of children in Britain. Chapter 2 provided sufficient documentation of that achievement: a half million children now benefit. Our research indicates that playgroups provide adequate care and, with continuing improvement in training opportunities being introduced, they will get even better. Britain has *already* developed the means of 'providing reasonable care for the many'. There is still a gap, however. More playgroups are needed. They can be helped to organize by encouragement from Whitehall and from local authorities, by both moral support and by such concrete aid as space in schools as it becomes available, bulk buying privileges, encouragement from local advisers and from Her Majesty's Inspectorate, and so on. But whatever means of aid and support are devised, they must honour one critical feature of the playgroup movement: it is a *volunteer* movement and its spirit and mode of organization as a volunteer movement affects not only the children looked after, but their mothers For the PPA and similar organizations have a role not only in preschool education but in community development.

One 'trouble' with the voluntary playgroup movement is symbolized by the dismissive remark that it is 'middle class'. In some statistical sense this is true. But one of the most vigorous playgroups studied in Oxfordshire was located in and catered for a working-class housing estate. Middle-class women have more of a tradition of volunteer work. But there is also a large element of self-help involved, and the present shape of playgroups fills middle-class needs well. Playgroup might flourish as readily in working-class neighbourhoods if they met needs there more realistically. Working-class areas are more likely to require a mix of full- and part-time care for working mothers. Might this demand be met by extended day playgroups with child minders associated with them as *aides*? Many community workers, volunteers, and local government officials believe that Britain has only begun to explore the diverse ways of providing care in a period of economic retrenchment. Imaginative innovation and diversification should be given all possible support.

Does there exist in Britain the means for addressing questions about the adequacy of preschool provision 'in a manner that is at once rational, compassionate, and economically viable'? How does one formulate *national* policy with respect to the preschool young? Obviously, one cannot dictate from above: it is simply inappropriate in a democracy such as Britain to prepare a rigid central policy statement on preschool provision or if it were prepared, for it to be funded or even if funded, for it to go unchallenged among local authorities. It is not how locally administered policies are made in Britain. But there is little point in evading the fact that there has been a traditional resistance in Whitehall to formulating *any* overall policies for the under-fives. It is no accident that, in the words of the CPRS Report, 'provision of services is fragmented and responsibility is divided'. The educational and social service professions – from Whitehall down to the local delivery of services – have no established tradition of collaboration. But it is not a lack of awareness on the part of both civil servants and ministers that produces such fragmented policy making. Indeed, there have been two DES/DHSS Circular Letters in recent years on the subject of coordination of services: one in March 1976 and the other in January 1978. What could be more 'conscious' than the statement on coordination in the 1978 circular: 'No services for young children and their families can operate in isolation; almost everyone working in this field has much to gain from the expertise and experience of people in other statutory, voluntary, and community services.' The Circular even goes on to urge closer collaboration with parents: 'Parents' knowledge of, and concern for, the needs of their own children need building on, not replacing; furthermore, parents have a vital role to play in their involvement with the services provided by voluntary organizations and as a result of community initiatives.'

Yet, the recommendations set forth in the 1978 Circular are as weak as ever: advisory committees at local level responsible to both Education Committees and Social Service Committees, but *without* executive powers – 'based on the belief that joint committees for the under-fives with executive powers could cut across important existing links – for instance between nursery schools and primary schools, and between services for children and for families as a whole – with damaging effccts'. In the end, the circular letter invites local authorities to submit examples of coordination for wider dissemination.

Scepticism is not often a constructive attitude, but it seems a fair guess that local authorities are not going to turn their under-manned staffs topsy-turvy with daring proposals if there is no material benefit to be gained. There *must* be an incentive for formulating plans, and the incentive can only be that the plans stand some chance of being funded, if only as pilot projects as in the Urban Aid Programme. I would agree completely with the recommendation of the CPRS Report that the incentive would have to take the form of earmarked grants for a period of several years (to assure carry-through), awarded to reasoned programmes submittcd for support. The sums of money need not be great, particularly if it wcre recognized that the period ahead should be one of explora tion and piloting against thc day when the economic climate permits fuller expansion and richer rcvision. This is not to say that the final pages of the DES/DHSS Circular Letter of 1978 do not contain excellent examples of local coordination between education, health, and social services. It is only that such effects do *not* counteract the decline of morale in the child care professions created by a series of cutbacks. Let the period ahead be viewed instead as one of experimentation for the future.

But the experimentation should by no means be restricted to the local level. There is an equally urgent long-term need for coordination, for getting it right at the higher administrative levels where the guidance of national policy occurs. It seems evident that this will not be effected by the present machinery of an Interdepartmental Committee that simply reviews departmental programmes over which in the end it has no authority. If the magnitude of the problem is as sketched in the preceding pages (and as seen by the Central

Policy Review Staff) then what is needed is nothing less than ministerial intervention by a Cabinet Committee established to put the matter under careful and tough minded review. I see no other way of overcoming the inertia that has kept interdepartmental coordination at so bland a minimum.

This leads directly to a broader issue – public participation in the debate. The preschool network does not have the authority structure of the education establishment. There are no binding guidelines, no inspectorate, little hierarchical control by local education authorities. Rather, it is a set of loosely connected and autonomous small units. Each child-minder lives within the circle of her own household, her friends, her extended family. Her relevant contacts outside that sphere are few and often off-putting – as when she decides to register and undergo inspection for safety, space, and suitability. There is no sisterhood of shared occupation among minders. They are not professionals in their own eyes. Their services are an extension of their domesticity. An association of childminders is only now coming into existence and the BBC has recognized minding for the first time with a series of programmes. Day nurseries undergo closer inspection and monitoring (even when they are not State nurseries) than do minders but they rarely turn outward for ideas and practices. There are few or no career lines in the world of the day nursery and, again, it is the rare nursery staff member who considers herself a proper professional. Indeed, in all Britain there is no graduate course for people in the day-nursery profession. They are nearly as poorly organized as minders.

The principal genius of the playgroup world is in the zest and autonomy of its local PPA groups to whom the parent organization provides point of view, training, and advice via a magazine like *Contact*. National PPA remains at a discreet distance: it neither formulates policies for local groups nor attempts to change practice by any save indirect means. Nursery schools and classes have a more organized place in the educational structure, but they too go it alone a good part of the time. BAECE, the association of nursery school staffs, has a not much bolder profile than PPA, with a newsletter, workshops and annual general meetings both by county and nationally. But schools do not have a close contact with the Local Education Authority on whose financial support they depend. Their network includes an adviser connected to the county or borough office. Yet, for all that, it is the head of each nursery who wields the greatest influence in her school and advisers do not often have much influence.

The conclusion that I draw from this state of things is that if there is to be a change in national policy, it will have to be brought about not only by reorganization of services at the local and national levels, but also by widespread public discussion among those affected. There is wide interest in the issue and a great deal of common sense that can be counted on among parents, community leaders and voluntary organizations. If there were to be a five year period of reorganization and experimentation, then every possible means should be used to broaden the discussion so that it may be brought into the communities affected. I say this with full appreciation of the controversial nature of provision for the care of the young – whether mothers should work, whether preschools should teach or simply provide an opportunity for play, how the financing should be allocated as between the public and private and voluntary sectors, and so forth. If it is argued that such public discussion might prove divisive and that it would further politicize the issue of child care in Britain, the answer would have to be that the risk is worth taking.

I say this for two reasons. The first grows from the conviction that most of the imbalances and inequities that exist and that are so vividly set forth in the CPRS Report are perpetuated precisely because the problems of child care are in effect kept under wraps and out of range of public discussion. The present degree of public accountability is, I believe, far too low. Nor, in fact, need fears of divisive debate be exaggerated, for surely it is possible to maintain a degree of flexibility and pluralism in public and voluntary provisions that would reduce fears that a singular policy was being imposed from on high and on political or ideological grounds.

The second reason is more important and deeper. Preschool is an extension of the private world of child care. The transition from the private and familial to the more public sphere of preschool is necessarily hazy. Parents are not willing (nor should they be) to give over complete control to the playgroup or the nursery school. The family is still the reference point. For all that he is away a few hours a day, the child is a member of *this* family: a Smith or Jones, a little Highlander or Yorkshireman, a member of one social class or another. To give over control of the young child entirely to experts or professionals is to give up not only privacy but a sense of one's own autonomy. Yet, in Britain as in America, where the Carnegie Commission on Children (Kenniston, 1977) has just reported widespread feelings of helplessness in families with small children, parents want more outside help. Nonetheless, they resist bureaucratic definitions of the kinds of help they should have available.

No long term benefit could accrue by making early preschool care seem like the exclusive domain of professionals. It would surely have a corrosive effect on the self-confidence of parents and reduce volunteer efforts. There has already been too heavy an assault on self-confidence – as witness the widespread belief that parents do less for their children's language development than the preschool, which runs counter to the burden of work in developmental linguistics (see Snow and Ferguson, 1977; Tizard, 1979).

One needs to ensure that parents keep confidence in their own skills as child rearers. They must be encouraged to feel that they too can have a large and expert hand in raising their own children. This is surely justification enough for stimulating more public discussion as part of an effort to reappraise policy towards children and families. Issues like child benefits, tax relief, job security and patterns of male and female employment must be part of public discussion. Preschool provision for the children of working mothers must come near the top of the list of issues to be discussed, but it would be in error, I think, to polarize discussion on that or any other single matter. So much of the present debate has centred on single issues, one at a time, that perspective has been lost.

One final point. There is no use hoping that a quick solution can be found to the problem of providing adequate and sufficient preschool care of young children away from home. The problem is too tangled and too neglected for that. Rather, it is a question for the longer term, one of mobilizing balanced resources to meet new needs and new priorities. 'Single-crisis' issues divert attention from the longer-term problem of providing the balanced provisions that the nation can afford. If Britain were to frame a policy and a pro-gramme for children within the perspective of a decade or even a quarter century, the cause of children would be far better served. The wild swing of contending policies would be damped. There would be less dealing with historical trends as though they were mere accidents of personal choice – like women working or mothers feeling depressed in the isolation of child rearing. Nor would there be so much cost: as in arguing that nursery education is a luxury when both major political parties have already committed themselves to nursery education. Let us set some reasonable goals for the middle range. There is need for careful thought and an experimental spirit. Shrill partisan debate serves little. Bri-tain is in a position to help herself through a crisis by a mix of voluntary effort and statutory support – a mix for which she is renowned. When the nation puts its mind calmly to the issues and looks with a clear eye to the changed world in which children and families live today, a successful policy will emerge.

Some tough-minded administrator might get the impres-sion after this lengthy recital of the shortcomings in care for the under-fives in Britain that, since things are not working well, it would be a mistake to throw good money after bad. Should the nation invest in care that is so far short of perfection? Does it make any difference what policy is adopted, given that none of the provisions is living up to the highest hopes of the 'experts' on the nurturing of child development? There are two replies to such self-defeating tough-mindedness, one moral and the other practical. The moral one is that nothing corrodes the confidence and morale of a people more than the feeling that it is failing to do its best for a next generation. Britain, like the rest of the Western world, may be sobered by the endless difficulties in achieving a new Jerusalem, but to give up the more modest goal of creating a workable society that can cope with the difficulties would be morally suicidal.

The practical reply is more obvious still. The conditions of modern life – its urbanization, the changed conditions of the family and of women particularly, the altered economic situation – all point to the importance of providing some community care for children before the age of school entry. It is not self indulgence that has brought the preschool provisions into existence for children between three and five – or even two and five. Provisions have come into existence to serve a need. The full-time care of children at home in the family in the years preceding school is neither desirable for many families nor, given that fact, is it good for children. Indeed, it can by now be taken as certain that an opportunity to be away from home in a preschool helps the child develop socially, intellectually, and emotionally. No less important, it helps the family as well – whether by making it possible for a woman to work if she wishes to or has to, or simply by letting her have the time she needs away from the lonely pressures of childrearing. More women have to work, as sole bread-winners. More women want some relief from the tasks of looking after young children. And more women wish to be part of the wider society by continuing to work after their infants have reached the age of three. A democratic government has the responsibility either to change the conditions that produce these views (and make plain what it is doing in order to achieve that end) or to see that provisions are being made to meet the new needs wisely and fairly. Britain is doing neither of these things.

The practical issue becomes plainer when one looks at the

positive side. If preschool experience – even in its present imperfect form – helps children develop, and helps them fare better in school later, how much more so would it do that given an improvement in the present provisions. But this is putting the case far too abstractly. We know a good deal about how to improve preschool provision, how to make it more interesting and challenging and humane. That is what this book, and the series of which it is a part, have been about. We are going through hard times economically. Yet, as I have urged, this may be the seed time for working out ways to give young children a better start and their families more heart in the future. It would not be costly. The return in kindling human hope for the future would be great.

Appendix
On collaborative research

There remains one last set of conclusions to set forth, and these have less to do with the nature and improvement of provisions for the under-fives in Britain than with the question, introduced in the Preface, as to how research findings may be disseminated in a form that is useful to practitioners. Obviously, one 'writes it up' and hopes that the books will reach the appropriate audience and in a form that will be relevant. And obviously too, books about the care of children *have* at times been relevant and even influential.

We thought it might be worthwhile, once launched on our research, to bring in as collaborators practitioners from the community to work with us so that we might learn from them what they felt they needed, and how our research might be modified to meet their needs. We were, I suppose, products of our times, eager to avoid a 'we' versus 'them' relationship between researcher and practitioner. But there were also some compelling reasons beyond the spirit of the times. After all, the principal expansion in British preschool care had come by voluntary effort on the part of such organizations as the PPA. They had not only set up more than 10,000 playgroups, but also organized their own training and tutoring schemes. They were practitioners, yes, but not professionals with the ordinary access to research knowledge that develops in a professional hierarchy like the educational system. We were also convinced that an informed body of parents, whether volunteer workers or not, was a good guarantee for the future quality of preschool care; their influence as informed critics would be invaluable. Moreover, the times seemed right for change. 'Received doctrine' about the education of young children was waning in influence and the social changes in family and community recounted in Chapter 2 were leading to a new thoughtful-ness.

Dissemination by collaboration

Our aim was to find some means of working collaboratively with practitioners in a way such that as ideas and findings emerged from the work, they could be tried out in practice, sent back for more research if found wanting, and so on. We wanted dissemination to continue in as close contact as we could achieve to the research as it happened. Our final report would be books about the research, to be sure, but they would also contain an account of how the research had fared in application.

We were in search of joint ventures. We chose to operate in the part-time playgroups and nursery schools since they were more organized and it seemed easier. Though we had already chosen a topic – the child's concentration and what affected it in the preschool setting – there appeared to be many ways of linking that topic to the concerns of the preschool people with whom we were making contact. Their practical problems would provide a context in which to explore our more theoretical interests.

The lessons they taught were, in the main, fairly obvious. One of them is that such collaborative research between a university-based research group and practitioners in the community requires an investment of time and resources that is difficult to come by in the lives of both. Research in Britain is rarely the full-time occupation of university dons, nor can practitioners take the time necessary for collaborating with them on mutually interesting problems. The don wants to get on with it and use his limited time 'effectively' – which means doing 'standard', publishable research rather than spending long hours 'just talking' about other people's problems.

Nor were we mindful initially of the suspicions that are generated by a venture such as we were proposing. Partly these were substantive: were we being too 'cool' and cognitive in our focus on children's concentration? Partly they were political. Were we being critical of present preschool practice? And partly there was an issue of status: were the university people sufficiently respectful and appreciative of the ideas and intuitions of playgroup leaders or nursery teachers? These were issues that could not be circumvented and we shall meet them in more concrete form in the pages that follow.

There were also problems of political and economic reality. If a collaborative effort collides with a political event, the former inevitably makes way for the latter! One of our most interesting 'failures' in the planning stage was the effort (initiated by the Senior Adviser of the L.E.A.) to establish a pilot nursery/playgroup in a large housing estate with a high concentration of single-parent families – at Neithrop on the outskirts of Banbury. It would have been an ideal venture from a practical and a research point of view. Unfortunately, the timing of this ideal project coincided with an economy drive in the County Council's Education Committee, and the money needed to expand the nursery service in the infant school of the housing estate never materialized. It is a workaday example, yet it serves to point a moral. All of the research we undertook existed in a political context that served to constrain it and, indeed, to shape it. Collaborative research aimed at aiding dissemination is risky research when it concerns politically sensitive issues. And preschool provision is a sensitive issue in a period of restrictive educational budgets.

Eventually a collaboration emerged. It was slow and sometimes painful.

The collaborative observation project

Our organizing seminar (see Preface) led us to choose as a central issue of our research the topic of *concentration*, a child's capacity to deploy his attention usefully, flexibly, without excessive distractibility. The choice was both practical and theoretical, and had considerable consequences for our later collaborative efforts. The reasons for choosing this focus were fairly obvious.

Concentration and distractibility are particularly sensitive indicators of a variety of conditions affecting children. For one, they reveal whether a child has 'got into' absorbing tasks, or whether he is bored or in over his head. Highly concentrated activity suggests the child is finding satisfaction and challenge in a task. Distractibility suggests trouble of some kind: social, psychological, or whatnot. Not much is known about what sorts of activities promote concentration. These are by now familiar issues (see Chapter 5).

I think that there is also a more indirect reason why we, researchers and practitioners together in a seminar, chose this focus. We, the researchers, had reached a justifiable scepticism about 'received wisdom' in nursery care. There seemed to have developed a nursery ideology of extraordin ary dogmatism. It rested on a strikingly narrow interpretation of what was referred to in a preceding chapter as the 'development idea' – that children must be allowed to develop in congruence with their own needs and modes of thought. In its most exaggerated form, this ideology translated itself into ideas about how nursery play should be organized. In general terms, it should be unstructured, spontaneous, and undirected – with materials such as sand, water, clay, and finger paints and with adult participation held to a minimum. The objective was 'expression'. Interestingly, the research literature on play seemed quite at odds with these views. It showed that one way of prolonging and concentrating the play bouts of children, for example, was to provide them with play material of challenging *structure*. (Our own research has confirmed these findings since.) Had it not been only a generation earlier the still admired Maria Montessori had made much of providing the child with structured materials to challenge his discriminatory and constructive abilities? And as for the role of adults, research by a member of our own seminar group (Dunn, 1977) had shown that a responsive adult not only increased the length of the child's play bout whilst the adult was present, but the effect persisted to lone play afterwards. The child seemed to be learning to organize his own activities through interacting with an adult. The nursery dogmas did not, on close inspection, seem very convincing.

The banning of adults had also led in many nursery schools to a silent ban on 'scripted' games, games with rule structures as in rounders or hide-and-seek. Yet the impression of William Kessen and the group of American developmentalists visiting the schools and nurseries of China with him was that children were not only *able* to play such 'scripted' games, but seemed to get an enormous amount of pleasure in concentrating their skills playing them, and, the while, picking up such necessarily scripted skills as turn-taking, appreciation of different roles in a game, keeping tally of the progress of an activity, and so on. Our scepticism about the received wisdom of total spontaneity was probably further reinforced by the preceding two decades of work on early intellectual, linguistic, and social development in children. The work of Piaget, of Vygotsky, and indeed of my own research group, pointed increasingly to the importance of rather intricate forms of 'rule learning' – whether in physical activity, in social interaction, or in the use of language. 'Child centred' nursery education seemed to us to be arbitrarily if benignly over-protective, to be turning its back on these challenging and new findings. It was not our intent to sell alternative views about nursery education, but to bring them into discussion as and when our research pointed us that way. We designed a method for observing play in nursery schools and playgroups that would not overlook such matters, while at the same time doing justice to the expressive side. Perhaps our hidden agenda was to raise consciousness among practitioners.

We had decided (see Chapter 5) to observe one child at a time for a twenty-minute stretch, using as neutral a category scheme as possible, one that is standard in field observation. We hoped to begin our collaboration by trying out this schedule with the aid of practitioners who could help us develop it and judge its usefulness. The development of a technique for observing children's behaviour seems obvious to the uninitiated. Alas, it is not. It is easy for systematic observation to miss the gist, to get lost in detail. It requires patient development. The collaborative development of this particular schedule told us much about the difference between doing 'ordinary' research and doing research 'in collaboration' with practitioners. To construct a good and reliable observation schedule is a highly professional, technical job. Its results, however, were to be of help to practitioners. We needed their advice if the procedure was to be useful to them in their work. We were able to arrange a working seminar of playgroup leaders, to try out and revise the observation method with them as collaborating observers.

Three or four of us researchers and six highly experienced playgroup tutors/advisors (led by the then County Chairman of the Oxfordshire PPA, Lady Phelps-Brown, who had handpicked the group) met regularly over several months.* Each of us would go into and observe some groups between meetings and then present the results to the seminar for discussion not only of what had been seen but how the observation categories worked. There was lively argument and some tensions as well. No question the seminar altered and improved the method. Inadvertently, the seminar also invented an approach to 'dissemination' that we never foresaw. The working seminar is worth a little description, for its history speaks to the opportunities and problems of doing collaborative work in the community.

Because the playgroup members were part-time workers, we were able to employ them not only to attend the seminars, but also to carry out trial observations in playgroups around the county. The pay was more symbolic than

* The members of the seminar were Lady Phelps-Brown, Avril Holmes, Sanchia Austin, Chris Wells, Ann Thompson, as well as Linnet McMahon, not part of the Oxfordshire group though a playgroup leader, and Kathy Sylva, Marjorie Painter, and myself from the OPRG.

economic, but it ensured that the members had time to work with us. I think it also indicated our 'seriousness', as did the participation of three of us from the OPRG who had worked on the observation method for months before. We soon learned how experienced a group we had with us. They made it clear what concerned them in the management of groups of children and in the kind of problems children had in playgroups.

We tried less successfully to set up similar seminars with nursery schools and classes. They were less successful, for protocol was immediately in evidence. Schools are institutionalized and 'statutory' in a way that playgroups are not. Heads had to be approached first, then teachers brought together for a meeting – after school, for teachers are full-time employed. Four seminars did form, and were led by Dr Sylva, but they were more 'instructional' than exploratory as the first one had been. It is difficult for full-time teachers to find time for making observations, though they finally did so in their own nursery schools or classes. And late afternoon seminars are not easy, sandwiched between demanding school duties and equally demanding duties at home afterwards. We did not offer pay, even symbolically, since the seminars were presented as training for professionals. Yet even at that, we had taken a step towards dissemination that was not clear to us until later.

We were approaching the end of our first year. We were just getting an inkling of the training possibilities of the observation schedule in the hands of teachers, a point to which I shall return in a moment. Word of the work had spread. I was invited to address the Annual General Meeting of the Oxfordshire PPA. I presented sample findings from our observations that might pose interesting questions to group leaders. There were already some interesting ones – like the surprisingly brief contacts between children and playgroup leaders, or the amount of child 'cruising' from one activity to another. We were still thinking principally of disseminating of *findings*.

The year ended. The autumn produced new demands:

getting on with observational studies by our own staff, starting seminars with the nursery teachers, beginning new projects. We were to encounter our first lessons in the human difficulties that can be generated when researchers and practitioners, each proud of their own skills, work closely together. During the summer I wrote a brief OPRG *Newsletter* (No. 4, 1977), describing our 'participatory' research with practitioners. But what had looked like joint participation to me, did not look like it at all to Lady Phelps-Brown, who was on me like a flash to remind me it was *our* research not theirs; that they (the PPA collaborators) had not been consulted as to aims. It passed. But it is worth mentioning, for it suggests some of the difficulties involved in attempting to share and diffuse knowledge by the kind of joint participation we had attempted to set up. A year after, Dr Linnet McMahon, a colleague on the Project, wrote a perceptive memorandum about the problem.

It seems to me that many of the Oxford Preschool Research Group's difficulties arise out of differing views of the meaning of participatory research. I am aware of two approaches, each with different expectations. One approach to participatory research consists of practitioners working side by side with researchers, jointly planning the direction of study and both feeling free to take initiatives. This has not happened in the OPRG and probably has not been intended to happen. Some practitioners may have been disappointed that this approach was not used.

Many practitioners may be quite happy to work with a modified approach to participation in which the researchers have a dominant role, deciding on policy, lines of approach and taking initiatives. (This does not mean that the researchers are not influenced by what practitioners have said.) The practitioners have a subordinate role in responding to ideas, even if their response is voluntary and even if it is fruitful in producing more ideas. In this situation the communication can be two-way, but the initiation of communication is one-way, so the onus is upon the researchers to keep the lines of communication open. In particular when researchers' policy or line of study changes, this and the reason for it must be communicated clearly to practitioners so that they do not feel hurt and think that they have been found wanting. This is particularly important in the preschool world because both nursery school teachers and playgroup leaders, as well as childminders, have anxieties (for different reasons) about the way others perceive their role and feel that it is not sufficiently valued. Compare the situation with that of a playgroup leader and parent. Here the parent has the lowest status. The playgroup leader must constantly think: 'Whom have I offended this week,' or 'Whom am I likely to offend,' and 'What move should I make first?' (It is no accident that playleaders' most insistent demands on an advanced field-work course is for more study of how to work with adults.)

Practitioners may well enjoy and benefit from working with researchers who may have something to offer them, as long as it is clear what the social structure is. If the practitioners' role is not clearly defined they will feel uneasy. One can compare their role in relation to the OPRG with that of an *au pair* girl in a family. She is supposedly the 'daughter of the house' but in practice her role is not that and she is uncertain what it is. General warmth from the family is not enough in itself to clear up doubts about where she stands.

In particular, practitioners will be upset and angry if it is made to appear (in reports, etc.) that they are working side-by-side with researchers when in fact this total participation does not exist. They feel put in a false position and made to look stupid, the unwitting victims of 'insertion' and intervention. In particular, they object because it then appears that they share the aims of OPRG when in fact they may not. They may have other aims or questions to ask which they have not had a chance to express.

Yet, for all the little difficulties, some unexpected things were happening as progress continued on the observation schedule. It was taking on a new function. It was not just a means of obtaining *findings* but a training device as well for playgroup leaders and nursery teachers. One of the members of the seminar (Avril Holmes, who later joined our staff part-time while serving as Vice Chairman of the County PPA) noted in a memorandum at the time that the schedule

(a) forced people to define their ideas in terms of behaviour everybody could see and agree on

(b) focused attention on continuities in what a child was up to

(c) was a good way of checking more quantitatively on one's impressions

(d) gave a sharper focus to key facts about behaviour – like the amount and kind of adult-child interaction

(e) And finally, liberated staffs from the usual clichés and labels.

Soon several practitioner members of the seminar proposed introducing it into their PPA foundation courses to sharpen observational skills. Indeed, 'observation' had always been a feature of PPA and nursery training, and the schedule fitted nicely into that framework. Soon, the schedule was put into a form explicitly designed for play leader training, complete with training manual, exercises, and illustrative examples. A research tool was doubling as a training instrument. *Observing Children* (Sylva, Painter and Roy, 1979) and its guide (Holmes and McMahon, 1979) are now publications of the PPA and in March 1979 the West Midlands Region of the PPA held its first workshop for tutors in Birmingham on 'learning to observe', using the new method as its base. Discussions were started with the Training Committee of the National PPA to explore how the instrument might be adapted for nationwide use, and the schedule for distribution has been published.

Is there any useful generality in this interesting turn of events? If an observational method deals with real phenomena in context – in this case, how children actually play in a natural group – it *should* be useful to the practitioner who deals with children in such groups. Yet there is an interesting anomaly here. It was our experience that simply *telling* the *findings* of research obtained with the observational method does *not* arouse much interest among practitioners. We found out the hard way. An opportunity arose for us to take over four weekly in-service training sessions under the joint auspices of the Oxford BAECE (the nursery group) and the Education Department. Playgroup leaders and nursery teachers attended. Each of the four evenings concentrated on different factors that extend the child's concentration: different kinds of activities, different materials, other children, participating adults. Those among playleaders and nursery teachers who had used the method as part of their *own* work, were interested. The others, in the main, were bored or bewildered by the statistics. So far as they could see, our numbers had nothing to do with their children. It was only when we left statistics – as when Dr Sylva spoke with the authority of a former teacher about the absence of games in playgroups – that the audience livened up. The newsletter of the Bicester PPA carried the following item after the series ended:

> In February we attended the four lectures given by Professor Bruner's Preschool Research Group. Although one could understand what the research was about, much of the language used was very technical, and each lecture appeared as lists of statistics. One was left wondering which playgroups they could possibly have visited. It was stated that throughout Oxfordshire there was zero rating for organized games, ie. no child in their observations played *Ring-a-roses* or *Farmer's in His Den*. During the first three lectures neither of us could grasp the purpose of this research work. We could not understand what value the outcome would have on the future development of playgroups.

For all that, some seventy loyal people showed up at each of the meetings in the dark of January and February 1977. They obviously were eager for help – and a modest proportion of them signed up for training in the observation method. But they were not, in the main, interested in our 'findings'.

Perhaps I have gone into excessive detail about the child observation project. If I have, it is because I find the narration necessary to illustrate *our* experience in 'giving psychology away' and to draw one generalization from it. In the realm of child care where one is dealing with concerned people, new knowledge *about* children that comes from *outside* one's own experience seems to make little headway against received wisdom and 'commonsense' practice. It is only when the research helps one to see with one's own eyes that it gets beneath the skin. The lesson I draw is that what matters is not learning *from* psychologists, but rather becoming a better one oneself – in this case *learning how to observe what children are doing*. 'Observing' is a curious form of activity. We know from a century of research on perceiving and observing that as ordinarily practised it is fraught with the perils of prejudice. When we are casually observing others, we pick up bits and pieces of their behaviour that fit our expectations and our preconceptions. It took us in our Project nearly two years to discover that the essence of dissemination was not in disseminating a *product* but a *process*, helping *them* to see more dispassionately rather than broadcasting what *we* had seen. It is not that our findings were not interesting (the reader can judge that for himself). Rather, what seems to matter is that our collaborators, the practitioners, should become participants in the process of knowing about children rather than mere spectators of the products of that process.*

Ideally, we should now test the effect of observational

* As this volume goes to press, BAECE has invited Dr Sylva to present our observational procedure to its 1979 National Annual General Meeting and another of our collaborators, Ms Carolyn Roy, has been invited to discuss it at a special workshop for preschool workers in the United States.

training on subsequent teaching. The project did not last long enough. Moreover, had we asked our teachers and playgroup leaders to become our guinea pigs in that way, there might have been no study at all.

Learning to observe children more systematically and in closer detail, however useful it may be to teachers, is still a long remove from the task of supervising their activity. The observer is, by definition, removed from those being observed and her influence on them is minimized. The heart of the matter in supervising or teaching children is to have some effect on them and to know what that effect is and how to modify it as needed. That was the objective of our second collaborative project.

Self-observation of teachers

Besides observing *children* in nursery groups from *outside*, we looked at them as well, recall, through the playleader's or teacher's eyes. It was a project with a background.

In 1970, David Wood (who was then a post-doctoral fellow with me at Harvard) coaxed me into a study on the conditions under which tutoring helped young children solve problems. How does an adult tutor actually help a child and how does the child manage to take up the help proffered? Our subjects, by happy coincidence, were threes, fours, and fives, and in due course the study was completed and published (Wood, Bruner and Ross, 1976). We discovered that any teacher, tutor, aide, helps a child by comparing what a child is actually *doing* with what the tutor's 'theory of performance' tells her the child *could* or *should* be doing. She (the tutor) then designs help in a *form* the child can appreciate and at an appropriate *time* helps him fill a gap in his actions. It was quite plain that the tutor's way of operating depended upon her theory about the child-in-the-task. And there were different 'styles' by which adults helped young children fill the gap.

It was with these ideas that Dr Wood's research began. It soon grew beyond this point. For he then raised the question of what happens when a researcher *discusses* with a teacher her ways of helping children fill their gaps – particularly when the discussion is based upon the teacher's observation of her own practice. A highly experienced head of a nursery school had complained that our child observations did not take sufficiently into account what teachers were *trying* to do. Dr Wood's approach was an attempt to get at just that question – to examine whether teachers and group leaders were accomplishing what they were trying to do and how they could better succeed in their efforts. It began a new chapter in our efforts at collaborative research that had its own dissemination built into it.

The final procedure he developed was described in Chapter 5. We ask a teacher or playleader, recall, if she would record a fifteen-minute session of her teaching on a miniaturized tape recorder in her pocket – any fifteen minutes at any time at her discretion during the playgroup or nursery school session. The recording is then transcribed and coded by the researcher. Teacher and researcher go over the coding together, teacher commenting particularly on what *she* was trying to do, what *she* thinks a child was up to, and so on. This is compared with a 'research interpretation' based on the coding system in terms of behaviour coded. It is *not* an effort to evaluate the teacher's performance. The object is to look both at a *participant's* account of what has been happening, and a sympathetic *spectator's* account, the researcher's. The brunt of the discussion between them is about how the teacher's expectations and intentions worked themselves out in her interaction with the child. How things work out from the spectator's view is in the actual numbers yielded by the coding of the session – though most often the teacher has a clear sense of what went right and what went wrong just from reading the transcript. But the counting and coding help. For coding brings things into cool and manageable proportions. It casts into relief the teacher's procedures in handling children: who initiates contact, over what topics, what is the talk about, how does the encounter close. Teachers often asked whether they might do another recording and discussion. Sometimes the researchers asked them. Many repeated, some as many as five times.

Dr Wood managed to obtain the part-time research collaboration of a teacher at a local nursery school: Martha Kempton, who had been a student of his on the child development course at Nottingham University. *She* served as the first subject in the experiment as well. It proved not difficult for her to induce other teachers to help her as subjects. That doubtless came from her being a teacher herself, but it is not unrelated to teachers' appreciating a trustful opportunity for reflecting on what they are doing. Mrs Kempton eventually returned to full-time teaching. Her place was taken by Dr McMahon, an experienced playgroup leader and a trained psychologist. She was then joined by an even more experienced playleader-tutor, Yvonne Cranstoun.

Very soon the research procedure itself rather than its findings began to arouse interest among playgroup and nursery people – again as a method of training or refreshing teachers. Eventually, County PPA officers asked to explore with us whether a research grant might be got to continue working after the termination of the present Project. As of the present writing, grant applications have been submitted to foundations by Dr McMahon and Mrs Cranstoun under the sponsorship of the Oxford Department of Social Administration. That is the story in brief.

Here was our second venture starting as research that turned into training. The result was not surprising but there is an administrative irony to all this that tells much about the pigeon holes into which research councils sort the world. We applied to SSRC, our sponsors, for a small supplemental grant to pursue the training implications of this work. The grant was turned down on the grounds that ours was a research enterprise, not a training one! In this instance the research requirement shot down the opportunity for working on dissemination.

Some remarks on collaboration

Perhaps there are a few points about dissemination via collaboration that grow out of these accounts. Ours was probably a typical experience of academics discovering the real world. We found our constituency of practitioners not surprisingly more interested in developing *their* skills than in hearing about our findings. When the latter could affect the former, the metabolism of collaboration picked right up. We published an occasional newsletter distributed quite widely to people in the preschool community. The letters of inquiry we received were mostly about the *participatory* aspect of the research; few asked for data tables to substantiate hints about what our research was uncovering. It was not that they wanted to participate with *us*, but rather to get into something of their own. Again, we met, in 1978, a few times with a group at BBC Radio London who were broadcasting discussions on the care of children. Their listeners, they said, wanted to hear from 'practical people' who had solved problems like those they faced themselves, rather than experts setting forth the state of the art.

All this suggests that 'dissemination' is the wrong metaphor for making research useful in the practice of child care. It smacks of spreading the word to the uninitiated. There is an increasingly educated population emerging who want to do better *themselves*. They do not want to be made to feel helpless or ignorant by experts; they are interested in cultivating skill. There is presently no available way of gearing child research into this effort of self improvement in child rearing.

However, the typical academic project is financed for two or at most three years by a grant from a research council. It is a grant to a university lecturer who, in addition to all else, has his university duties to perform. His future may hang on getting a piece of publishable research completed in that time. Working collaboratively with practitioners in a way to improve *their* effectiveness is slow. It rarely results in the elegant paper so favoured by learned journals. There is rarely a reward for community achievement. Research councils are not often in the business of practitioner training. There are very few research centres in Britain concerned with the transformation of research findings into practitioner skills – as, for instance, the teaching hospitals are. In the field of development, the Thomas Coram Foundation in London (concerned with social, psychological and economic issues in the field of early childhood) is an exception. It would surely be worth the time, the effort, and the finance necessary for activating other centres with comparable objectives.

It is of interest that in recent years there has been a freshened interest in the study of human development and particularly in developmental psychology. There is an increasing number of applications for study and the largest fraction of psychological research grants now goes to this field. It is a field that has nurtured investigators in Britain of world renown – Susan Isaacs, Anna Freud, John Bowlby, Jack and Barbara Tizard, Michael Rutter – who have ventured beyond the laboratory into the rich and conflict-laden world of child care. The younger generation of developmentalists – in Britain as in the United States, France and the Soviet Union – is lively in its interest in the manner in which the context of environment affects social, emotional and intellectual growth. There is widespread readiness to explore ways and means of turning the research process to social ends. That readiness needs to be exploited in order to bring psychology in Britain into practical service for children.

Within the community of practitioners there also exists a new readiness for entering into collaboration with academics – but not as junior partners or research assistants or, simply, as consumers of findings. This readiness is attested to by the training courses of volunteer organizations like the PPA, by the emergence of courses at colleges of further education, by the popularity of new courses in child care at the Open University. There is also, as already noted, a good deal of ambivalence towards 'experts' who are seen to be pontificating – whether in fact they are or not.

How to build a bridge between the two? The obstacles are still very great. So long as the rearing of children (by parents or others) is seen to be the 'mere' expression of instinct, concepts like training, sensitivity to children, and the like, will be dismissed. This was a problem in trying to figure out ways to help childminders to do a better job (see Chapter 6). But as already noted, there is an equal and opposite problem when parents or intending *aides* in childrearing become convinced that the expert professional must be approached for advice hat in hand.

Rather the answer (difficult though it may be to achieve) lies in recognizing that bringing up children requires not only natural or instinctive sympathy for them, but that it can be enriched by knowledge about children and intelligence in its application, and made more effective by the cultivation of skills. The skills are not obscure: they are of the order discussed in Chapter 5, and involve principally some recognition of the effects of one's own response to children on the minds of children – whether in talking, doing things together, or sharing feelings.

There may be coming into being a new profession concerned precisely with turning knowledge about human development into skills for cultivating its development. The demand in many countries that research carried out in this institution or that school be justified in terms that have to do with aiding human growth is often described as a form of anti-intellectualism. It may be, rather, evidence of a lively consciousness of what knowledge is for. Detached research – using the children of this or that school as subjects in experiments without concern for the problems of this or that school – can still be justified in an abstract way. But in the end, this or that school cannot be denied the right to ask who is helping *them*.

In the concluding chapter, just preceding, I proposed that a national discussion on child care and its support be initiated as part of a programme of revising and improving present provisions for children. One aspect of that discussion will surely involve the universities, the colleges of education, the

research councils, and the preschool community. It is precisely how to bring about joint research and training that
maintains a high intellectual standard on the research side
yet ensures the provision of practical training for those in
charge of the care of the young.

The first nation that manages to resolve this persistent
problem will, I think, become the new Jerusalem!

Short Bibliography

ANDREWS, C. L. (1979) *Tenants and Town Hall*. Department of the Environment Social Research Division, Housing Development Directorate. London: HMSO.

ASSOCIATION OF COUNTY COUNCILS (1977) *Under Fives*. London: ACC.

BARKER, R. G., and GUMP, P. V. (1964) *Big School, Small School*. Stanford, California: Stanford University Press.

BENNETT, S. N., JORDAN, J., LONG, G. and WADE, B. (1976) *Teaching Styles and Pupil Progress*. London: Open Books; Cambridge, Massachusetts: Harvard University Press.

BLACKSTONE, T. (1971) *A Fair Start*. London: Allen Lane.

BLANK, M. (1974) *Teaching and Learning in the Preschool: a Dialogue Approach*. Columbus, Ohio: Merrill.

BONE, M. (1977) *Preschool Children and the Need for Day Care*. London: Office of Population Censuses and Surveys.

BROWN, G, W and HARRIS, T. O. (1978) *Social Origins of Depression*. London: Tavistock; New York: Free Press.

BRUNER, J. S. (1977) *Newsletter* No. 4. Oxford Preschool Research Group.

BRYANT, B., HARRIS, M. and NEWTON, D. (1980) *Children and Minders*. London: Grant McIntyre; Ypsilanti, Michigan: High/Scope.

CENTRAL POLICY REVIEW STAFF (1978) *Services for Young Children with Working Mothers*. London: HMSO.

CENTRAL STATISTICAL OFFICE (1977) *Social Trends*. No. 8. London: HMSO.

COMMUNITY RELATIONS COUNCIL (1975) *Who Minds?* London: CRC.

CORNWALL SOCIAL SERVICES DEPARTMENT (1974) A look at childminding. Research and development study No. 9. Unpublished.

COURT REPORT (1977) *Fit for the Future; the Report of the Committee on Child Health Services*. London: HMSO.

CROWE, B. (1973) *The Playgroup Movement*. London: Allen & Unwin.

DEPARTMENT OF EDUCATION AND SCIENCE (1972) *Education: a Framework for Expansion*. London: HMSO.

DEPARTMENT OF EDUCATION AND SCIENCE and DEPARTMENT OF HEALTH AND SOCIAL SECURITY (1976) Low cost provision for the under-fives. Papers from a conference held at the Civil Service College, Sunningdale.

DEPARTMENT OF EDUCATION AND SCIENCE and DEPARTMENT OF HEALTH AND SOCIAL SECURITY (1978) Coordination of services for children under five. LA Social Services Letter LASSL (78) 1 Health Notice HN (78) 5. DES Reference S47/24/013.

DUNN, J. and WOODING, C. (1977) Play in the home and its implications for learning. In Tizard, B. and Harvey, D. (eds) *The Biology of Play*. London: Heinemann Medical Books.

FINER REPORT (1974) *Report of the Committee on One Parent Families*. London: HMSO.

GARLAND, C. and WHITE, S. (1980) *Children and Day Nurseries*. London Grant McIntyre. Ypsilanti, Michigan: High/Scope.

GARVEY, C. (1977) *Play*. London: Open Books/Fontana; Cambridge, Massachusetts: Harvard University Press.

GARVEY, C. (1976) Some properties of social play. In *Play: its Role in Development and Evolution*. Harmondsworth: Penguin.

GOODALL, J.v. L. (1971) *In the Shadow of Man*. London: Collins.

GRAVES, N. B. (1969) *City, Country and Childrearing in Three Cultures*. Denver, Colorado: University of Colorado Institute of Behavioural Sciences.

IMBER, V. (1977) A classification of the English personal social services authorities. DHSS statistical and report series No. 16. London: HMSO.

HARMON, D. (1977) A survey of policies for early childhood. Paper given at the Aspen Institute for Humanistic Studies, November 1977.

HOHMANN, M., BANET, B., and WEIKART, D. P. (1979) *Young Children in Action*. Ypsilanti, Michigan: High/Scope.

HOLMES, A.and McMAHON, L. (1979) *Learning from Observing*. London: Pre-school Playgroups Association.

JACKSON, B. (1973) The childminders. *New Society*. **26,** 521. 29 November.

JACKSON, B.and JACKSON, S. (1979) *Childminders*. London and Boston: Routledge & Kegan Paul.

JAHODA, M., LAZARSFELD, P. F. and ZEISEL, H. (1971) *Marienthal: the Sociology of an Unemployed Community*. London: Tavistock; Chicago: Aldine.

JENCKS, C., SMITH, R., ACLAND, H., BANE, M. J., COHEN, D., GINTIS, H., HEYNS, B. and MICHELSON, S. (1972) *Inequality*. New York: Basic Books; London: Allen Lane.

KENNISTON, K. (1977) *All Our Children*. New York and London: Harcourt Brace Jovanovich.

MAYALL, B. and PETRIE, P. (1977) *Minder, Mother and Child*. London: University of London Institute of Education.

McNEILL, N. and McNEILL, D. (undated) Linguistic interaction among children and adults. Memorandum to the Committee on Cognition and Communications, University of Chicago.

OFFICE OF POPULATION CENSUSES AND SURVEYS (1975) *Census 1971; England and Wales. Summary Tables*. London: HMSO.

PLOWDEN REPORT (1967) *Children and their Primary Schools; the Report of the Central Advisory Council for Education (England)*. London: HMSO.

RIESMAN, D. (1950) *The Lonely Crowd: a Study of the Changing American Character*. New Haven, Connecticut and London: Yale University Press.

RUTTER, M., MAUGHAN, B., MORTIMORE, P. and OUSTON, J. (1979) *Fifteen Thousand Hours*. London: Open Books; Cambridge, Massachusetts: Harvard University Press.

SINFIELD, A. (1978) The social costs of unemployment. In Jones, K. *Yearbook of Social Policy in Britain 1976*. London and Boston: Routledge & Kegan Paul.

SHINMAN, S. (1975) Parental response to preschool provision. Brunel University (Mimeo).

SKEGG, D. C. G., DOLL, R. and PERRY, J. (1977) The use of medicine in general practice. *British Medical Journal* **1,** 1561–3.

SHORTER, E. (1976) *The Making of the Modern Family*. New York: Basic Books; London: Collins/Fontana.

SNOW, C. E. and FERGUSON, C. A. (eds) (1977) *Talking to Children*. Cambridge: Cambridge University Press.

SPIRO, M. E. and SPIRO, A. G. (1975) *Children of the Kibbutz*. Cambridge, Massachusetts and London: Harvard University Press.

STACEY, M. (1960) *Tradition and Change: a Study of Banbury*. Oxford and New York: Oxford University Press.

SUOMI, S. J. and HARLOW, H. F. (1975) The role and reason of peer relations in rhesus monkeys. In Lewis, M. and Rosenblum, L. (eds) *Friendship and Peer Relations*. New York and Chichester: Wiley

SYLVA, K. D., PAINTER, M. and ROY, C. (1979) *Observing Children*. London: Pre-school Playgroups Association.

SYLVA, K. D., ROY, C. and PAINTER, M. (1980) *Childwatching at Playgroup and Nursery School*. London: Grant McIntyre. Ypsilanti, Michigan: High/Scope.

TIZARD, B. (1979) Language at home and at school. In *Language and Early Childhood Education*. Cazden, C. B. (ed.). Washington, D.C.: National Association for the Education of Young Children.

TOUGH, J. (1977) *The Development of Meaning*. London: Allen & Unwin.

TRADES UNION CONGRESS WORKING PARTY (1976) *The Under Fives*. London: TUC.

TURNER, I. F. (1977) Preschool playgroups research and evaluation project. Final report submitted to the Government of Northern Ireland Social Services Department. Queen's University of Belfast, Department of Psychology.

WOOD, D., BRUNER, J. S. and ROSS, G. (1976) The role of tutoring in problem solving. *Journal of Child Psychology and Psychiatry*. **17**, 2.

Index